"This is no quick fix, self-help bool
more valuable than that. With his ble
practice and personal pilgrimage, c
with contemporary relevance, Sunil I
probe our fundamental priorities and [illegible] encourages
us to face the why questions about the biggest and inescapable issues of our existence, of life and death, meaning and purpose. But it also charts an attractive path to a life of greater enjoyment, fulfilment and potential flourishing, which might just change everything. It is well worth examining. I warmly commend it."

David Jackman, Past President of the Proclamation Trust, London

"I often think about wise outcomes as a judge. I pray for wisdom in my legal work. Of course I need to know the law well. But without wisdom applying the law, the law can sometimes be empty, cold and unfeeling. Wisdom can be cultivated, can grow and be improved. Others invariably see wisdom before we may see it in ourselves. Wisdom is lifelong especially where there is so much else impinging upon our lives creating artificial priorities.

So I was really inspired by this book. It's never too late or too early to seek wisdom. The book is also in the tradition of the self-help genre, although we all need help in the cultivation of wisdom ourselves.

For Christians who find wisdom particularly as God given, this book challenges us as to the life and reliance on Christ. But this is a book for any person with openness of mind and keenness of spirit. This is no superficiality, glossy glib ideas, selfie lifestyle indulgence. To follow honestly this quest for wisdom requires honest endeavour. I was really impressed."

David Hodson OBE MCIArb, Solicitor (English and Australian), Mediator and Arbitrator

"Management training courses can usually be distilled into quick fix solutions on how to transfer knowledge, how to acquire skills or how to change attitudes. It is very rare to find any resource to help executives gain wisdom. In his book *Dancing with Wisdom*, Dr Raheja provides a path to overcoming life's trials, truths and frustrations in a way that encourages the reader to look beyond the superficial quick fix answers of our age to timeless truths of eternal significance."

Ram Gidoomal CBE, Chairman, Traidcraft PLC

"We all would like to be wise. Being clever, sharp or insightful isn't the same thing. Wisdom is a gift and has huge potential to change our life, our relationships, our world. Within these pages you have the opportunity to grasp this gift. You'll be wise to do so!"

Peter Kerridge, CEO, Premier Christian Radio

"Sunil's writing and teaching has been a massive, massive help to me for many years now. The depth and richness of Sunil's experience is hard to beat: he has worked as a psychiatrist helping some of the most marginalised people in our society; he is widely read and his writing is full of gemstones of wisdom from others; he has experienced life in a wide variety of cultural settings in both the East and the West; and, best of all, he has drawn on the deep truths of the Scriptures to give answers to life's questions.

A hallmark of Sunil's writing is that it is easy to read. His writing is full of examples and personal testimony. The beautiful dedication at the start of this book records that it provides the lessons Sunil would have loved to have shared with his friend Bunty, who was (before his death at a tragically young age) like a younger brother to Sunil. I am massively grateful that, in this book, Sunil has chosen to share those lessons with us all.

Finally, I should also add this: when you pick up a book you sometimes wonder if the person who wrotes it actually 'lives' what they write about. I've had the enormous privilege of knowing Sunil and his family for many years. The Sunil you meet in this book is exactly the same as the Sunil who you meet in person. If you're looking for a guide to accompany you in your quest for wisdom, he's a good 'un."

Dr Dominic Hughes, Barrister

"I've known Sunil for over a decade. We've met up regularly over that time and my lasting impression is how original he is and how fresh and striking his insights. And now to my delight I have found that experience of him in person reproduced in his book. I assure you, as you reflect on your journey through life and allow Sunil to sit alongside you in his psychiatrist's chair, you'll find yourself discovering a wisdom path through life's trials and frustrations, through its ups and downs to lasting meaning."

Rico Tice, Associate Minister, All Souls Langham Place

"A wise and compassionate, deeply enthralling piece of work, worthy of whole-hearted, clear-headed and serious contemplation—be prepared to be challenged! So many multitudes of mental health patients present to the NHS today crying out to us that their lives feel empty, suffering in the midst of feeling that their lives lack real purpose and fulfilment. So many of our patients struggle in knowing how to relate to themselves let alone to others. They ask, 'Where can we go for direction and guidance?', 'Is there really meaning to be found in this life that actually matters?' 'Can this meaning endure and is it worth fighting for?' Dr Sunil Raheja has, through the pains and tears of both his professional and personal experience, crafted a real gem of a book that unashamedly, clearly points and guides to an invitation that is beautifully irresistible to us all."

Dr Angharad Gray, NHS Community Psychiatrist

"We are used to 'professional advice' that helps us to get well, but Sunil offers us genuine wisdom that offers us transformation beyond our expectations. He writes with warmth, honesty and razor sharp insight."

Rev Will Van Der Hart, Co-Director
MindandSoulFoundation.org

"Sunil exposes Western secular thinking that dominates, or seeks to dominate, much of the world. He breaks the yoke of expectation and conditioning. His journey provides crisp, valuable insights to those seeking self-discovery and deepening wisdom."

Simon Lees, Real Estate Consultant

"Sunil provides a sure-tested path for the curious and hungry person to transcend the triviality and superficiality of our age to lasting meaning for your one and only life."

Tomas Brunegård, CEO of The Stampen Group 1996-2012; President of the World Association of Newspapers and News Publishers, WAN-IFRA, 2013-2017

DANCING WITH WISDOM

A Sacred Quest to Restore Meaning, Purpose and Fun to Your Life and Work

Dear Jasmine, Priya + Simran,

With love,

Sunil

SUNIL K. RAHEJA

Printed in the United States of America
Published by Author Academy Elite
PO Box 43, Powell, OH 43065
www.AuthorAcademyElite.com

Identifiers:

LCCN: 2020911880
ISBN: 978-1-64746-346-5 (paperback)
ISBN: 978-1-64746-347-2 (hardback)
ISBN: 978-1-64746-348-9 (e-book)

Available in paperback, hardback, e-book and audiobook

Book design by Jetlaunch. Cover design by Debbie O'Byrne.

CONTENTS

DEDICATION

This book is dedicated to Abhishek ('Bunty') Bannerjee 12 October 1981–17 March 2014.[1]

To a wonderful man who was both a dear friend and like a younger brother to me.

Gandalf, I thought you were dead. But then I thought I was dead. Is everything sad going to come untrue?

—*The Lord of the Rings*, J. R. R. Tolkien

1 Abhishek Banerjee was Bunty's official name. Growing up, family and some friends referred to him as Bunty. It was only at school and work that more people started using the name Abhishek. Both names are used interchangeably in this book.

Bunty, in Delhi on the evening of Saturday 15 March 2014, I gave you a big hug to say goodbye. I had no idea it was going to be the last time we would see each other. I look forward to getting another big hug when we meet again in eternity.

When I think back on our ten-year friendship, it is only now I understand what happened. Often you came to me as a younger brother looking for wisdom to deal with the difficult challenges and questions about your life.

This book on discovering, desiring, developing and deepening in wisdom provides lessons I would have loved to have shared with you. Without either of us realising it at the time, you helped me lay the foundation. As painfully short as it was, I thank God for our friendship.

> *Very truly I tell you unless a grain of wheat falls to the ground and dies it remains only a single seed. But if it dies, it produces many seeds.*
>
> (Gospel of John ch12 v24)

Dear reader, my prayer is that this book will help germinate a seed of supernatural transformation and change within your life, surpassing all expectations. Because Bunty had such a profound impact as a friend, it would be good to know and begin to make sense of his tragic loss, as this single seed produces many seeds.

It is my sincere desire for you to know a joy and fulfilment in life that can even transcend death. May this book play a part in your quest for wisdom. In a world of much meaninglessness and mediocrity, true wisdom can still be found.

> *Keep me from the wisdom which does not cry, the philosophy that does not laugh and the greatness which does not bow before children.*
>
> —Khalil Gibran

PREFACE

Life is not about waiting for the storm to pass; it's about learning how to dance in the rain.

—Vivien Greene

By the age of thirty-six, I had achieved everything I thought I wanted and life still felt empty. On the surface everything looked ideal, if not perfect. I was happily married for coming up to eleven years. A few months earlier we had celebrated the arrival of our third child. The senior position of consultant psychiatrist which I had been working towards for many years was now mine. I was a volunteer leader in a new church that I had helped to get started. Our financial future was secure. But in spite of all this, I found myself frustrated, restless and discontented.

I kept asking myself, *Where am I going and what am I achieving of any lasting significance?* The days seemed to rush by; and I felt that I was only going through the motions. It all seemed so pointless. At times everything felt exhausting. This is a common experience for many of us at some stage. Maybe it has been your experience. Perhaps you are feeling the same way currently. If not, then it is possible that one day this will be your experience as well. According to a 2020 study by the National Bureau of Economic Research, the worldwide norm is that unhappiness peaks somewhere around the age of forty-seven or forty-eight.[1]

On top of that, our lives are becoming increasingly complex, confusing and even contradictory. There is a gap between what we say we want to do and what we actually do. In spite of major technological advances, with the apparent progress which they bring, we often appear to be drowning in an ocean of averageness. We allow ourselves to be distracted and tranquillised by the trivial. Our phones send an alert, and we find ourselves briefly elated because someone has 'liked' whatever we posted on social media. Or we feel outraged by a thoughtless remark made five minutes earlier by a politician from the other side of the world. Along with this, many of our previously trusted institutions—like government and religious organisations—are now regarded with suspicion.

In our so-called post-modern culture, agreed upon values are increasingly deconstructed and discarded. The Internet Age encourages the viral spread of outrage and abuse while at the same time discouraging respectful discussion. Social commentators tell us that we live in a post-truth culture where opinions are more important than the facts of a situation. Feeling as though we are drowning in a sea of superficial priorities, many of us long for something more meaningful. We need something both rationally and intellectually credible, something emotionally and existentially true and satisfying. The global pandemic of 2020 forced many of us to reconsider which parts of what we live for have lasting significance.

At the same time, living a life of significance appears to pass us by. Socrates said, 'The unexamined life is not worth living'.[2] What does that say about us, who live in the most over-informed and under-reflective civilisation in human history?

What we need is not more of the same but timeless truths, which can connect with the best version of who we are and who we long to be. The word for that is wisdom. It comes not to the most fortunate, or intelligent, but to those most determined to find it.

Welcome to your quest for wisdom. Such a quest will inevitably change you and leave you never quite the same again. It can also start you on the greatest adventure of your life so far.

Whatever your age or background, whatever your past or your experience, whatever the disappointment or setback, your best days do not have to be behind you. They lie ahead of you.

Following a path towards wisdom can turn the bad into the good, prove that good things are never quite lost and show you that the best is yet to come! Instead of frustration, you can discover delight. In place of a deep-seated sense of meaninglessness, you can find purpose. And rather than life being exhausting, it can become an exhilarating adventure. What would it mean to have that without the hangover of guilt, shame, or embarrassment? Yes, even our life with all its hidden wounds and broken dreams has the power to transform. If we are alive and breathing, then it is still not too late to bring to life that eternal calling buried deep within us. This is a dance on the edge of mystery and glory to a life that exceeds our capacity to measure or control.

It is my honour to welcome you to this sacred quest for wisdom.

INTRODUCTION: WHY DISCOVER WISDOM?

Discovering and Walking Along the Road Less Travelled

Don't wish it was easier, wish you were better.
Don't wish for less problems, wish for more skills.
Don't wish for less challenges, wish for more wisdom.

—Jim Rohn

"Will this book make me rich?" Possibly. Possibly not. "Will it help me find the life partner of my dreams?" Maybe. Maybe not.

"Will it help bring the lasting happiness, fulfilment and contentment which we all long for?" Ah. Good Question. I would love it to do exactly that!

Above all those good things, there is a challenge which I am throwing open to you. My challenge is to open your eyes to see that the foremost need in your life is wisdom. Yet, knowing the importance of wisdom is not enough. My aim is to encourage you to develop wisdom as the thread with which all your life is woven; a life which will soar above just surviving or going through the motions. May I share with you a deep desire to show that there really is a path to the enduring success, significance and abundance we all long for. This is very different to the path signposted by disappointment, frustration, anger, sadness, depression and cynicism. That path characterises the world as it affects us now. Such cynicism poisons souls, and a toxic soul finds fault in all that is around us. A negative, dark filter lets in no light.

If I could summarise the essence of what wisdom is about and how it can directly impact your life, it would be the answer to these four simple but profound questions. The answers are the cornerstone foundations of a new life:

1. Being

If I am going to be a person I can live with, then what kind of person am I going to be?

2. Relating

How do I relate to others – my family, my friends, my work colleagues, those who come into my social orbit, the wider global village? What is an appropriate way to relate to them? Where do I find the healthy balance between sober seriousness and the fun in life?

3. Doing

"My life will be meaningful". What kind of work will achieve this?

4. Leaving

What legacy do I want to hand over as my life comes to an end?

For most people, these are questions we rarely give time or attention to. Yet they are always at the back of our minds, waiting for meaningful answers. Wisdom provides solid personal answers to those simple, but penetrating questions. It is also the constant guide beside you for the rest of your life. The more you feel secure about your answers to those questions, the more that wisdom will permeate your life. The more you grow in wisdom, the more fulfilled your life will become.

And, you will have fun along the way!

HOW I CAME TO WRITE THIS BOOK

When a stranger discovers that I am a psychiatrist, almost inevitably I will get a comment such as "Are you able to read my mind?" or "Are you analysing what I am thinking?"

Well, I can confidently say that is definitely not the case! The psychiatrists I know and work with tend not to do such things! However, I have always been interested in people. You could call me nosey if you like, but I've always been fascinated by whom people really are beneath the surface of how they appear to be when in front of me. My work as a psychiatrist and personal leadership coach has given me a privileged position to get to know many people on a deeper level. It truly is an honour to have people share with me things they have never spoken about with another human being. Maybe there is an unspoken fear or regret, or maybe there is the germ or seed of an idea that is brought out into the open for the first time. It's a genuine privilege to be with someone over time and see that fragile idea or inkling become a solid and integral part of their life. I get to see them take those first fitful steps from fear and insecurity to deep joy and quiet confidence in life and what it may or may not bring.

What I have also noticed is that someone may look confident and very accomplished on the outside, but when I get to know them, I find all sorts of fears, self-doubts and insecurities. Similarly, another person can seem quiet and soft-spoken, but as I dig deeper, I find a steel-like determination. They are clear and focussed on who they are and where they are going. They may even be ruthlessly focussed on achieving what they want. Appearances can be very deceptive!

My own story is that at the age of eighteen, I went to university to study medicine so that I could become a doctor. I had a vague desire to enter a career in which I could help people. While I was very good at mathematics and the sciences, I could see no point in a career that I could not say, without hesitation, was clearly helping people. And that was the main reason I chose to go into medicine! When I look back at my naïve eighteen-year-old self who made that decision, I have to laugh at my foolishly simplistic thinking as well as my lack of imagination!

However, when I began studying medicine, I became deeply disappointed and frustrated. For me medicine came across as being only concerned with treating people as machines—knowing all about, for example, their anatomy, biochemistry and physiology. Don't get me wrong. We need people who know those things. It was simply not what I had signed up for, and it didn't fit my personality or temperament.

I chose to endure the training over six long years even though the only exams I could pass for the first time were the Finals!

I found the experience of medical training deeply traumatising, especially in the first year. The relentless learning of facts and having to memorise so much information became exhausting and draining. However, it also brought a profound spiritual awakening that over all the years since has never left me. We'll come to that later in this book.

A few years afterwards I found my niche in psychiatry. I entered a speciality where people were more than machines to be poked and prodded or have blood taken from. It was a discipline concerned with understanding how someone thinks, fears, worries, or becomes anxious, as well as how they function at work or in their families and even in society at large.

I have worked as a psychiatrist focussing on people with learning disabilities since 1999 (That is the last century!). I have found this section of the population to be the most socially disadvantaged group in society. Statistics around the world repeatedly show no other group has worse health or social care outcomes. Right across life, from being at increased risk of intrauterine abortion to then becoming marginalised, abused and exploited by others who are more able, they are truly among the most vulnerable members of society. Yet for much of the time, they are hidden from our awareness or presence. By and large, they are often ignored by society and popular media. That is unfortunate, as so many have important stories to tell.

I have also regularly been deeply touched and at times in awe of the love, care and devotion shown by many parents for their adult children who are unable to do even the simplest of things for themselves. Along with the challenges in looking after this vulnerable group of people, there are also the additional concerns of possible abuse and neglect by others. But those with learning disabilities are an important part of our society.[2]

As time goes on, I have been struck by how limited is our understanding of people when they are seen only as a 'disease model'. In psychiatry, we study conditions such as schizophrenia, dementia and bipolar affective disorder in detail. Those are important subject areas, but they are only one limited part of the human experience. We are much more than the diseases and illnesses that affect our minds. That is why I have developed a deepening fascination with positive psychology and how different people can be from each other. Looking at, and finding, myself at times struggling in an increasingly changing and challenging world, I have been intrigued by what makes people different from each other. I boil it down to three overlapping questions:

1. *Why do some people grow and develop in their lives in incredible ways*? In a parable given by my favourite teacher in my favourite book, this growth and development is in terms of a harvest which becomes ten, twenty, or even a hundred times more than what was sown. It is truly awe-inspiring how productive some people's lives can be. What do these people do that the rest of us do not do, will not do, or cannot do?

2 For more on this, see the video *A Message to a Scared Future Mother* at drsunil.com/dearfuturemum

2. *How are some people not just productive, but also at peace with themselves and others?* Like a fine wine, why do these people evolve to become sweeter and more lovable with age? That is by no means an automatic maturing process. In fact, and more often than not, the reverse is frequently the case. With advancing age can come an increasing self-centredness and self-absorption along with a complaining negative cynicism. Some people can achieve so much with their lives, but the vast majority discover that it is at a cost to something that is also very important to them—for example, their health or their family. Why do some people not just achieve incredible results but also have great relationships and personal contentment?

3. *How do such people think, feel and behave to flourish so well in their lives?* For those who manage to get it right—and there are relatively few of them—what is their difference in thinking, emotions and mindset compared to the rest of us?

My interest in such questions has also led me to develop a private practice which combines mental health, personal and team development paired with coaching. I seek to help my clients go from the confusion and complexity of their lives—often manifesting as undue worry, anxiety, stress, depression, burnout, or ADHD—to resilience and whole person flourishing. Their future becomes much more exciting and rewarding than anything in their past.

To develop and deepen my exploration of this more, I have been blogging and podcasting on the theme of what it means to make sense of life in an increasingly challenging and complex world. The title of my podcast on iTunes is *Dancing With Wisdom (Making Sense of Life).*

Much of life is focused on the externals, or the bright, shiny objects of apparent success. But time and time again, we see that external achievements do not fill or complete the aching void within our hearts. We long for more but cannot seem to put our finger on what it is that will ultimately satisfy and bring lasting fulfilment.

In some ways, we live in one of the best of times to be alive. For increasing numbers of people, compared to previous generations, we have never had easier access to improved health, opportunities and prosperity. The opportunities that the extraordinary advances in technology have brought us in the last twenty years are—if we stop to think about it—mind-blowing. And yet it seems that there has never been more unhappiness, stress and discontentment surrounding our lives.

It is with these fundamental changes in the nature of our lives that—to put it simply—I help my clients gain clarity from the complexity of much of modern life.

The problem is that many otherwise highly intelligent people sabotage themselves by becoming stuck in negative thoughts and habits. Such thinking can derail them and get in the way of reaching their deepest desires and aspirations.

I take the people I work with through a seven-part journey framework to help them understand what they really want. Through this framework, they are then equipped with the tools and skills to arrive there, or even somewhere better. That allows them to live their lives with a greater sense of purpose and direction, knowing the best, most exciting and fulfilling part of their life is not behind but actually lies ahead of them. When fully grasped, our life can literally turn around and bring a joy and zest for living which we may not have experienced since childhood. But, it won't come automatically.

We have to be deliberate in our focus. We need to be hungry for such a life, and we have to be intentional and purposeful in pursuing such a life. We also need to find resources of compassion and grace for ourself and others to handle the inevitable setbacks and failures that will come our way.

I sincerely believe that every person with a hunger for growth can thrive and find ultimate joy through life's many complexities, pain, disappointments and chaos.

We can turn our life around to live with greater clarity, meaning and purpose. And this book explains how to accomplish it.

WHO THIS BOOK IS FOR

This book is for you if you know you have a lot to give to the world but you repeatedly get in the way of your own progress. Maybe in the past, you blamed your parents or your upbringing. Maybe it was your work environment, those difficult colleagues, or the naysayers in your life. What you have come to realise, in fact, is that the greatest obstacles have actually come from within yourself. You discover you can't blame anyone or anything else.

Yes, we live in a challenging and complex world, but you have slowly and finally come to the conclusion, as Theodore Roosevelt once put it, 'If you could kick the person in the pants responsible for most of your trouble, you wouldn't sit for a month'.[3] You have come to the sobering and even discouraging realisation that you have participated in every bad decision you have ever made! While you may have been poorly guided or given wrong advice, you still chose to take the path that got you into the mess you find yourself in. It takes courage to come to that realisation. If you decide to embark on this journey, I want to commend you for being willing to explore such an uncomfortable truth. Many people never reach this stage.

How many times have we thought we need a change of circumstances? If only you were in a different job or lived somewhere else. Maybe if you were married to someone else or not married at all, maybe if you had children or didn't have children at all, or there is the guilt, pain and regret of a decision you wish you had never made that keeps coming back to haunt you. So, you find yourself living in the past. Maybe there is worry or anxiety about the future.

The problem with all this kind of thinking is you still have to live with yourself! You take yourself with you wherever you go in life! If you have made the first difficult step of seeing yourself as the person in your own way, then you will empathise with G. K.

Chesterton. He famously wrote to *The London Times* newspaper when they posed the question, 'What is wrong with the world?' His reply to this question was just two words. 'I am!'[4] If that resonates with you, then this book is for you. If it does not, then you can stop reading now and safely put it away.

I'm sorry to have to break the news to you, but in case you hadn't yet realised it, life is difficult! It is not easy. If you think it is, then sooner or later you are going to be in for a rude awakening. There is certainly much in the way of fun and enjoyment to be had, but life has its challenges and unexpected twists and turns.

How can I, in the words of Friedrich Nietzsche, confidently say, 'What doesn't kill me only makes me stronger?'[5]

WHAT QUALIFIES ME TO WRITE THIS BOOK?

I want to make this book as accessible and practical to you as possible. What qualifies me to do so?

First, I write as a psychiatrist who has spoken privately to a wide range of people from different backgrounds who have endured a range of difficult and tough situations in their lives. I have also seen how even though some people can go through basically the same experiences, their responses can be very different and lead to noticeably different outcomes. What are the things I have noticed and the patterns I have observed? This book includes some of them.

More importantly, I am writing as a human being who has lived life as a husband, father, son and as a friend to others. I have made many mistakes, and from my failings I have learnt and continue to learn. Some of these lessons I am going to share with you. I have written the book which I wish had been available to me when I was younger!

I am a lifelong learner and observer of human nature. My aim is to take you on a journey with me to help you unpack the potential and resources which are within you and available to you.

I had responsibility for the leadership of a non-profit organisation in a voluntary capacity over about ten years. Working in a team, and subsequently becoming burnt out towards the end of my time, taught me important and valuable lessons about myself, human nature and longevity. As I attempted to balance the different parts of my life, I found I did not like the person I had become. As painful as those lessons were, they taught me some things about human nature and myself that have had a deep impact on my life. I believe that these lessons can have a similar impact on the lives of others—without necessarily the same level of stress and turmoil that I went through. If this book can help you avoid or learn from some of the pitfalls I have experienced personally, then it will have been worth publishing.

We live in a world that is changing rapidly in many fundamental and profound ways. It can be hard to know what one should be doing and why. To help you navigate through this complexity, I should be honoured if you were to think of me as your Sherpa or guide for the hills, valleys and hidden dangers of this quest.

To help us, I am unapologetically going to call upon many different authors and writers who have gone before us. They provide valuable insights and perspectives for us as we set out on our own unique life travels. Their experiences may not have been ours, but there are certainly principles and hard-fought lessons we can learn and heed from. There are only two ways to learn—from your own mistakes or the mistakes of others. How much better to learn from the mistakes of others!

WHY YOU NEED TO READ THIS BOOK

WHY A QUEST?

Life is a journey, travelling along a road. Going down that road, we come across new people, changed circumstances and differing situations. Some of these are familiar, though most are not. No two days are the same, but each one can be testing. Think of your days at school. In school, you have the lesson and then the test. I've observed that in everyday life, it is actually the opposite. In life, it would seem to me you have the test first. It is not till you pass the test that you move on to the next experience or level in life.

I am sure you have seen examples of this in your own life or the lives of others. Have you ever noticed how some people get stuck with the same script? It is as though they are like a broken record playing the same tune again and again. For instance, they get into a relationship with someone. For a few months, it all seems to go well, as they are madly in love. Then, it suddenly goes wrong and that person has become a complete disaster for them. They are angry and bitter. They find someone else and the cycle repeats itself. Or they get stuck into a cycle of dysfunctional relationships at work. They seem to never get out of that same pattern of behaviour.

There is a helpful Old Testament way of describing this. 'The skills that got you out of Egypt are not the same that will get you into the Promised Land'. When the Israelites were slaves in Egypt, they had a miserable existence living in terrible hardship. After a number of divine encounters and experiences during forty years in the desert, they entered their Promised Land. Quite suddenly there was a whole new set of challenges to deal with. They had to learn a new way of thinking and living. The Israelites were on a quest that involved changing themselves as much as responding to different circumstances. The Biblical book of Exodus shows us that although it may have taken the Israelites one night to get out of Egypt, it took forty years to get Egypt out of the Israelites!

A quest is a long search for something which is difficult to find or is an attempt to achieve something difficult. This is not easy. If it were easy, then perhaps I wouldn't need to write a book about it. The process of writing this book has led to some fundamental changes in my own life. I am not the same person I was when I started. I have a greater understanding of my weaknesses, flaws and inconsistencies. I also find I am more gracious and compassionate with myself and others as well as more confident with the calling of my life. My aim is that you will have this greater sense of ease with yourself by reading this book.

A quest is different from an adventure. In an adventure, you go out on an exciting journey. It spices up your life, and then you come back home to pick up where you left off. By contrast, a quest is not something you choose. Rather, the quest chooses you. You are called to it because of what is going to be demanded of you. In many ways the person you are at the beginning never really comes back from a quest. Either you die on the quest or, if you do come back, you are so fundamentally changed that you are not the same person as when you set out.

My intention is that as you go through this book you experience something similarly life changing. There are some very important aspects of life at stake. Most at stake is the very person you are in the process of becoming. The French philosopher and Jesuit priest Pierre Teilhard de Chardin explained this in terms of understanding ourselves as 'not human beings having a spiritual existence [but rather] we are spiritual beings having a human existence'.[6] The implication is that every person we meet, no matter how seemingly ordinary, is on an infinite trajectory towards either dazzling beauty or terrifying horror. The sobering implication is that our personal choices and interactions with one another are in some profound and mysterious way taking us to one of those two destinations.

If we truly grasped the enormity of this, how could it not profoundly affect the way we treat one another in our conversations, behaviour and actions? Every human being is made in the image of God. Over time, this image is either becoming more radiant and glorious or being replaced with an opposite terrifying darkness, worse than anything a horror movie can imagine. We like to venerate nations, culture, art and civilisation as timeless. We are conditioned to believe that the end of our lives on earth means the end of our existence. But this is only the belief of our Western-style secular approach. This quest for wisdom takes our focus away from the finiteness of this world in the present moment, with all its beauty and its fractures, to an immortal view of human beings and creation. As C. S. Lewis described it:

There are no ordinary people. You have never talked to a mere mortal. Nations, cultures, arts, civilisations—these are mortal, and their life is to ours as the life of a gnat. But it is immortals whom we joke with, work with, marry, snub and exploit—immortal horrors or everlasting splendours.[7]

This quest we are on can have significant personal implications, not only for ourselves but also our family, friends and local community, as well as nationally and even globally. I trust this book will inspire you to take the higher and deeper path of personal transformation that will have a positive impact on you in the first place. From this beginning it will also have a beneficial effect on your family, friends, colleagues and all of those with whom you interact. Your life and choices matter, so why not strive for the best possible life? In the words of poet Mary Oliver, "Tell me, what is it you plan to do with your one wild and precious life?"[8]

WHY THE BEST?

Our world is obsessed with the best. Everywhere you look there is a fascination with the fastest, the richest, or the most beautiful. It is easy to feel inferior and deflated when there are so many who are way ahead of us and we can see no possibility of getting even remotely close to those ideals. But what if we could look at what we call 'best' in another way? What if the best was about being the best possible version of me? Such a perspective takes away the need for me to compare myself to others. I am not in competition with you, and you are not in competition with me.

This outlook is about growing and developing to reach our full potential. It is a combination of both character and behaviour. In much of modern life, character and behaviour are separated out into different compartments. What someone does in private is regarded as irrelevant (unless illegal according to the laws of the time) to how they conduct themselves in public. In recent times in Britain, we have had a Prime Minister who has been widely accepted as having the skills to run the country, even though he has been unsure of whether he has fathered five or seven children.[9] The United States has had a president who has faced numerous allegations of inappropriate behaviour with women.[10] This is accepted because private behaviour has been considered irrelevant to the ability to perform or accomplish results in the public arena.

By contrast, I firmly believe that understanding wisdom means the person we become is as important as what we are doing, how we behave day to day. To grow in wisdom is to move towards the best version of us, living the best possible life to which we are called. As we explore, it does not necessarily have to be in ways other people might define as successful or the best. Instead, the best possible life becomes one where we become all that God calls us to be and where we do all that God calls us to do. This is about a wholeness and integrity that extends to the core of our being. Of course, all of us fail in this every day, but is there a path of wisdom that can give us the courage and strength of conviction to pursue such a life?

TO GROW IN WISDOM IS TO MOVE TOWARDS THE BEST VERSION OF MYSELF, LIVING THE BEST POSSIBLE LIFE I AM CALLED TO.

In a world that is preoccupied with external appearance and charisma, we are challenged every step of the way. Yet we intuitively know how true it is. What is the point of having crowds love you when the reality is that you feel so empty and hollow with those closest to you? History has numerous stories of celebrities who have been adored and appreciated by the masses. Behind the façade, it later emerges how deeply they struggled. This conflict may have been with feelings of inadequacy, worthlessness, guilt, or emotional pain. In extreme cases this conflict has even led to suicide.

WHY WISDOM?

As a society, we are slowly realising that the significant problems we face are not due to a lack of information or even intelligence. In the past, we could say we did not have access to enough information. Thanks to the Internet and the other technology we have, that is no longer the case. We have more than enough information—maybe even too much information. The question is . . . what do we do with it? How do we filter it? How do we decide what is important and what needs to be discarded as not important?

There is also what is known as the 'knowledge-doing' gap. We know what to do and we know what is good for us, but we don't do it. We tell ourselves that we don't have the energy or the time, and deep down, we know that is not really the case at all. We tell ourselves we need to get up early in the morning at 6 a.m; when the alarm goes off the next day, we just want to go back to sleep! Or we tell ourselves we need to eat healthily, and then we see that delicious snack we know we shouldn't eat. . . .

It's possible that you're thinking that you should make your goal happiness or a trouble-free life. The problem is that this is something we can never quite achieve. The targets keep moving. The unexpected or unplanned happens and often derails or distracts us.

Many decisions, in order to make them well, only require knowledge. If we had all the knowledge, we could choose the right car, maybe the right medicine. Other decisions are mainly a matter of our principles and commitments. For example, we know it's wrong to steal and we know that we have a responsibility towards caring for our elderly parents. But for the vast majority of the decisions we actually face in life, the rules and the facts won't help us. The questions are never-ending:

- Who do we marry? Do we get married? Who should we date?

- Is this relationship actually good for us? Should we stay together, or should we break up?
- What career should we go into? Should we go into a business deal with that person?
- What school or university should we attend?
- Should we stay here? Should we go to another job?
- Should we move here? Should we move there?
- Should we confront the person, or should we hold back? Should we tell that person what we really think even though it might upset them?
- Should we take the risk, or should we play it safe?
- How do we handle our own mortality?

It's sobering to realise that a wrong decision in any of those situations could be a disaster, yet there are no clear rules to tell us specifically what to do. Whatever you think the moral rules are, they don't cover all these questions and knowledge simply isn't enough.

Through the power of the various media, it is Western-style secular thinking that dominates or is seeking to dominate great parts of the world. We live in a culture, based on scientific and secular values, which thinks scientific expertise provides all the answers. We are conditioned to expect to find natural (as opposed to supernatural) causes for everything we see and experience.

What we are learning at this point in history is that this Western-style secular approach does not give the answers to any of those questions I mentioned earlier. Nor does it answer the questions on our mind about most of the things we deeply need. Of course, there are religious people, those we might call moral people, who say, 'Morality is important'. I agree completely that morality really matters. It is crucial, but it does not help in those areas where the choice is not between right and wrong but between options that, on the surface at least, appear ambiguous. We need wisdom if we are to unravel this complexity.

The more that I have reflected on this, the more have I seen how so many people are literally dying from a lack of wisdom in key areas of their lives. They are held hostage by the triviality and sensuality of much modern life. This hurts not only them but also their families, workplaces, communities and all of our society. It is tragic that so much is preventable.

If science is organised knowledge, then wisdom is an organised life in the fullest sense of the word. A person who navigates life well is wise. They may not have all the answers or know what lies ahead, but they can look at life with a quiet confidence and assurance. A wise person lives life with boldness in spite of all the inevitable difficulties, uncertainties, challenges and setbacks. Do you hunger and thirst for such a life?

IF SCIENCE IS ORGANISED KNOWLEDGE, THEN WISDOM IS AN ORGANISED LIFE IN THE FULLEST SENSE OF THE WORD.

WHY IS WALKING IN WISDOM A QUEST FOR THE BEST POSSIBLE INVESTMENT?

Bringing these three elements together—Quest, Best Life and Wisdom—if the Best Life comes from living in Wisdom, should not that be something we hunger and thirst for in our life? The writer of the Old Testament's Book of Proverbs, simply referred to as Proverbs, says,

> *Choose my instruction instead of silver, knowledge rather than choice gold, for wisdom is more precious than rubies, and nothing you desire can compare with her.* (Proverbs ch 8 v10–11)

King Solomon wrote this in the 10th century BC. He has been described as the wisest person who ever lived, he was also the richest man of his time. It has been estimated that Solomon had an annual income of more than $50 million in today's terms. He lived in a palace that took thirteen years to build, owned 40,000 stalls of horses, sat on an ivory throne overlaid with gold and drank from solid gold cups. The daily menu of his household included 100 sheep and thirty oxen. Whatever way you measure it, that is unimaginably wealthy!

Yet Solomon still says that wisdom is more important and valuable than all of his wealth! Wisdom, Solomon would say, is still the best possible investment.

For our world today, which often appears obsessed with making money and getting ahead, Solomon's admonition is still a very provocative claim. Could it be actually true that wisdom is more valuable than a large pile of money or the objects and experiences that we might yearn for? Could learning to walk in wisdom put you and me on a quest for the best possible life?

To grasp and understand this means re-evaluating our priorities. It will require humility and courage. But maybe even more; it will require an on-going hunger and thirst to explore what fundamentally lasts.

I have come to the conviction that only through a deep interior life with God can a person truly fulfil their divine purpose and calling. I have also concluded that the highest form of wisdom is found in Biblical scripture. I was not brought up on the Bible but came to read it seriously for the first time at the age of nineteen in the autumn of 1984. Since then, I have continually been in awe of its ability to penetrate and analyse not only my own behaviour and inner motives but also much of human psychology. I do not mean to say that insight is not accessible in other places or from other religions, spiritual traditions, or from disciplines like psychology. However, I find myself returning to the Biblical Scripture and discovering so much which resonates with what it means to be human. I have experienced how much God speaks through the Biblical revelation; as a result this revelation has become the basis of my life and faith.

You do not have to share my faith to benefit from this book, but I invite you to explore my quest with your own life and experience. I will be making significant references to various parts of the Bible. Originally written in Hebrew (most of the Old Testament, with some sections in Aramaic) and Greek (the New Testament), there are a variety of different English translations which I quote from. I invite you to sample these quotes and see how much they resonate with your own experience.

My invitation is to join me on this adventure of inside out transformation!

WARNING

While I am a psychiatrist and medically trained doctor, I need to be clear on a few points. Nothing I say or write here constitutes specific medical advice. You are the expert on you. I do not know your specific life circumstances, so I cannot take responsibility for any consequences or results that may come from reading this book. My desire and prayer for you is that the wisdom you encounter in this book will lead to transformation in your life which is radical and positive. I would love to know how this book has helped you. Feel free to contact me at the accompanying website at dancingwithwisdombook.com.

I am also a disciple of Jesus Christ, following a profound spiritual encounter in my late teens. You can watch a fifteen-minute video on that at drsunil.com/me.

This spiritual encounter and the life that I have led since has governed and guided so much of my life. Even so, you do not have to have a current belief in God or Jesus Christ to benefit from this book. I am certainly going to make plenty of references to what God has done in my life and could also do in yours. You can find a great deal of help from what is written here regardless of which faith background you come from, and whether or not you have a background of faith. I leave you to make your own decisions and conclusions about what you read here. In many ways, the only requirement for deriving real benefit from this book is a genuine hunger to grow and to see lasting change in life.

My intention for you after reading this book is that you will have a hunger to live for God in a deeper and richer way, wanting to make an eternal difference with your life in whatever your God-given calling is.

If you have questions about the existence of God and evidence for why you should believe or trust him, then I can direct you to the following books I have found particularly helpful:

- *The Reason for God*—Tim Keller
- *Making Sense of God*—Tim Keller
- *Mere Christianity*—C. S. Lewis
- *Confronting Christianity*—Rebecca McLaughlin

As you work through this book, you will find that I will be including more and more material on how it is only God who can enable and empower us to live a life of wisdom. I make a number of Bible references.

If you are quite certain and have no doubts that God does not have a place in your life and is irrelevant, then this book is probably not for you. If you put yourself in this category, may I invite you to reflect on the historical trend in faith and belief. It is certainly the case that in the past 100 years of recent history that there has been a significant decline in those identifying themselves as religious in both Western Europe and North America. However, on a global level, not only has religion failed to decline but sociologists are now predicting an increasingly religious world. These are sociologists from the same school as those who only a few decades earlier confidently predicted the end of religion in the world.

It is true that numbers do not explain everything. But projections by the respected Pew Research Center suggest that in 2060 Christianity will continue to be the world's largest belief system, increasing slightly from 31% to 32% of the world's population.[11] During this same time period, it is predicted that Islam will have grown substantially from 24% to 31%. Hinduism is set for a marginal decline from 15% to 14% and Buddhism from 7% to 5%. Judaism will hold stable at 0.2%. Perhaps most interestingly, by 2060 the proportion of the global population identifying themselves as atheists, agnostics, or having no faith will have declined from 16% to 13%. This book does not go into any detail about the reasons for this. At least some of this change is due to those who are religious having more children. However, an important consideration remains that many people simply do not believe the secular worldview is able to provide the answers which they seek in a world confronting them with increasing complexity, change and uncertainty.

For several decades, many who do not believe in either God or religion have confidently assumed that as society advances and progresses, their secular view would also be increasingly ascendant. The Pew Research Centre statistics suggest otherwise. They also suggest that those who do not believe in a role for either God or religion would benefit from reviewing this approach. If this applies to you, I would suggest this alternative worldview is well worth consideration. I would even say that you owe it to yourself, and those around you, to at least understand why so many people feel a need to turn to a divine perspective on wisdom in their lives.

This book is not an exhaustive breakdown on everything to do with wisdom. It is too vast a subject to encapsulate in a single publication such as this. What I have drawn together here is the best of my thinking to date about principles and applications to help you hunger for and grow in wisdom in your own life. One of the challenges with writing a book on such a subject is the fact that your thinking is recorded. Although your perspective and what you emphasise may change over time, the book is still there to remind you where you were before.

I am also not a theologian or someone with any formal church role. Any authority I may have comes from my favourite book, the Bible. This book is the world's number one bestseller. It is also one of the most poorly read and most misunderstood books ever published. If you are unfamiliar with how to interpret Bible references, I have included an explanation at the beginning of the Notes section of this book.

Wisdom is not about what you know but who you know, and how these personal, intimate connection points open sources of wisdom. For me, I am continuing to learn and grow in my understanding of what it means to walk in wisdom while being in a relationship with the living God through His son Jesus Christ.

I would very much like you to join me with where I am currently. I would suggest you go to my blog at drsunil.com and my podcast *'Dancing With Wisdom (Making Sense of Life)'* on iTunes. I am planning also to include additional resources at dancingwithwisdombook.com.

This book is designed to be an experience for you to first ponder on, then experiment with and reflect on. From that point, I would encourage you to take the principles and lessons you need to apply to your own life and challenges.

TWO GUIDING PRINCIPLES

As you read this book, we will be guided by two principles:

First, I certainly do not intend to cause offence to any person or group of people. Every individual is uniquely valuable, with the right to hold and express their opinion so long as they do it in a considerate and respectful way. As mentioned earlier, I have worked with people with learning disabilities for many years and one thing this has shown me is the importance of showing respect to everyone regardless of their abilities, opinions, or beliefs. Every human is equally valuable simply because they exist. If anything written here offends you personally, then it certainly is not my intention.

My second guiding principle may be more challenging. Opinions and ideas are not all equally worthy of the same respect. Some ideas (such as human beings are intrinsically valuable) can be respected more than others (such as the earth is flat or one race, religious group, or social class is somehow superior to another). The problem is that it can be very hard to separate our opinions and ideas from our personal identity or even our very being. It is easy to feel that if our view or idea is challenged, then our identity is being challenged. It is very easy, consciously or subconsciously, to leap from saying, 'Because you think my view or opinion is stupid' to then assume 'you think that I am intrinsically stupid'.

Psychologists talk about how our default way of thinking is to make decisions for emotional reasons and then try to justify them logically. A few hundred years ago, Thomas Cranmer expressed this as 'what the heart loves, the will chooses and the mind justifies'.[12] What this means is we have strong emotional attachments to our opinions and ideas. These attachments are often stronger than logic or external evidence. We have what is known as a 'confirmation bias' when we hear new information. It means that we tend to focus on those facts which confirm what we already think and dismiss the rest. Often we are not aware that we are doing it, but we have a habit of more easily recalling which facts we find favourable and forgetting ones that do not appeal to us. If we are challenged, our natural reaction, rather than reflecting on the message we hear and its implications, is to 'shoot the messenger'. Especially if the topic is emotionally charged, we instinctively find ways to attack the person bringing us this new perspective or truth. There is a very important point to make here. Rather than blaming others when you are challenged, I encourage you to examine your own heart and decide what could apply to your own life. You will gain the most from this book if you are hungry to learn and willing to be challenged about some opinions and beliefs you thought were self-evident and not in need of challenging.

That is the way we all grow—by venturing out beyond the comfort zone of our own understanding, our blind spots and self-limiting beliefs. We learn to acknowledge where we have gone wrong and are prepared to change direction.

Think about our analogy of travelling between two places. We all want to make progress to our intended destination. If we take a wrong turning, then we will not progress to the destination by stubbornly carrying on along that road. If our destination is a city in the north, then taking a road south will only take us further away from where we want to go. In this case, to make progress we have to turn around completely in order to get back on the right road. Whoever is most able to turn around to get back on the right road is the one who will see most progress. But, to turn around you need the humility to accept and acknowledge that you have taken the wrong road. Getting back on that right road is the quickest way to get to your intended destination.

Progress in wisdom will come from facing the uncomfortable truth that both personally and as a society, we have taken wrong turns in many areas of life. This is easier said than done. I know. Just ask my wife when she wants to give me directions and I am convinced that I know better than the map that she wants us to follow! While we like to think of ourselves as logical and rational we often react to situations, and especially the unexpected, in emotional ways.

The limbic system is the emotional part of our brain that is activated when we feel threatened. In the distant past, it served as a helpful function to enable us to react quickly to predators or physical danger and flee to safety. We develop a limbic system reaction when we feel our idea or opinion is challenged. We stop thinking rationally and develop a so-called 'fight, flight, or freeze' reaction to protect the identity or ego which is so tightly bound to the person whom we think that we are or should be. Either we shut down emotionally and refuse to get involved in a conversation with someone we disagree with, or we find ways to attack and demean the other person. From a neuroanatomical point of view, we need to allow our maturer prefrontal cortex to think about the issues raised in a more logical and rational manner.

One way in which we instinctively avoid doing this is with what is called chronological snobbery. This is the assumption that, only on the basis that something is old, it must be obsolete and unnecessary. This is a frequent feature of current thinking, yet one that proves most unhelpful. Various media outlets, for example, conduct surveys on a topic or certain idea. Statistics are confidently given as to how popular this new idea is. It becomes clear that it is not the strength or logic of any argument that matters, but rather that it must be accepted solely on the grounds that it is the latest idea. There is little in the form of careful analysis, or a desire to understand why an old idea has gone out of fashion. For example, was the idea ever refuted as untrue? Who challenged the old idea, where was it challenged and how convincingly was it set aside? Or did it decline like a passing phase? If its disappearance is indeed the result of change and time, does that tell us anything about its inherent truth or validity? Writing on this in the 1940s, C. S. Lewis said:

> *From seeing this, one passes to the realisation that our own age is also 'a period,' and certainly has, like all periods, its own characteristic illusions. They are likeliest to lurk in those widespread assumptions which are so ingrained in the age that no one dares to attack or feels it necessary to defend them.*[13]

I am reluctant to be drawn into a detailed discussion on specific examples. But changing views over the last fifty years on differences between religions, on abortion, assisted dying, gender identity and acceptable sexual ethics all illustrate this chronological snobbery.

To walk in wisdom is to have a hunger for asking questions about life in ways we may not previously have done and for developing the humility to explore the answers. Rather than, unquestioningly, accepting whatever is the most popular view, we can benefit immensely from understanding why and how particular ideas have been accepted or rejected. As we develop this understanding, we will find the strength and courage to live the life we were created to live. We will be less distracted by passing fads and fashions that lack substance or lasting fulfilment. The challenge is to live as we have been called to be and to become the person we are intended to be. Nahum of Bratslav expresses this powerfully and, to my mind, with great beauty.

When I appear before the Heavenly tribunal and I am asked, 'Why did you not lead your people like Moses?'

I shall not be afraid.

When I am asked, 'Why were you not a David who worshiped me and shepherded your people?'

I will be calm.

When they query, 'Why were you not Elijah who spoke the truth and brought forth justice?'

Even then I will not shake.

Ah, but when they ask, 'Nahum, why were you not Nahum?'

It is then I will tremble from head to toe![14]

Can you sense what is at stake here? It is about discovering and living all that we were intended to be, with awe and with wonder.

As we become more comfortable with the person we were created to be, we can focus on the work we were intended to do. As we do so, not only will we be fulfilled but we will also bring a positive contribution to the world.

Work such as this fulfils four important criteria:

- It is work that gives our life meaning.
- It is work that lets us be our best self and helps us become a better version of ourself for the benefit of others.
- It is an unparalleled pleasure when it goes well, and is worth fighting for when it goes poorly.

- It is work we are willing to organise our life around.

How different would our world be if more of us had this perspective on our lives and sought to grow and develop ourselves and our work in such a way? It would create a virtuous circle of positive action and emotion, powerfully transforming our world for the better.

Are you ready to start this important and exciting quest?

OK. Let's begin!

We are going to start with what was a defining moment in my own life.

REVIEW QUESTIONS TO CONSIDER

1. What have been pivotal or life-changing moments in my own life?
2. "The greatest need is not a change in circumstances but a change in perspective." How well do I see this for myself ? Do you agree or disagree?
3. How hungry am I for this wisdom?
4. King Solomon claims in Proverbs that "Wisdom is more precious than rubies, and nothing you desire can compare with her?" How much do I believe this? Is that a credible claim to believe?

PART 1

Desiring Wisdom

We do not receive wisdom, we must discover it for ourselves, after a journey through the wilderness which no one can make for us, which no one can spare us.

—Marcel Proust

1

WISDOM FOR THE HEART

I think that taking life seriously means something like this: that whatever man does on this planet has to be done in the lived truth of the terror of creation...of the rumble of panic underneath everything. Otherwise it is false.

—Ernest Becker, The Denial of Death

17 MARCH 2014

Her panicked voice at the end of the phone made time stand still.

"If somebody's heart stops beating for three hours, can they still be alive?"

It was eight in the evening on Monday and one of my daughters had handed the phone to me. She said that it was Abhishek's wife, Jayshree. It was odd, why she should ring me at what would be such a late hour in India. I had spoken to Abhishek that morning, thanking him for his friendship and hospitality. I had been in Delhi for a week and arrived back in England on Sunday evening. Before leaving for London on that

Sunday morning, I had been with Abhishek (Bunty) the night before until well past midnight.

"When you get to London, Sunil, I want you to ring me."

"Bunty, that will be well past midnight your time!"

"I know. Even so, do ring me."

It was a strange request. But he was very insistent, so I agreed. I gave him a hug and said goodbye. As he reversed his car very close to a wall, I made a joke. Bunty was always quick to look at the funny side of things. But this time, he said nothing. His face was serious. I waved goodbye. And he was gone.

My flight landed in London on Sunday evening. It felt so good to connect again with my wife, Sally, and our children. It was a bonus that our friends Isaac and Gloria were also staying with us. There was much to catch up on and get back to now that I was home. I looked at the clock and remembered my promise to Bunty. It was past 9 pm—or 2:30 am in Delhi. I remember thinking what a ridiculously early time it would be to call someone in India. But I had promised Bunty. I knew that at times he was something of a night owl and he had been insistent.

So I rang. Not surprisingly, no one picked up. The next morning, Bunty returned my call, but I was driving, so I had to postpone our conversation. I promised to call back within a couple of hours.

I called back and we exchanged some pleasantries. I also asked my daughter, Nisha, to speak to Abhishek that morning to say thank you for the unexpected gift of an SLR camera he wanted to give her. I had casually mentioned a few days earlier that she was becoming interested in photography. The next time I saw him, he suddenly presented it to me. When I had protested to him about how unnecessary it was, he quickly explained that it was his old camera which he no longer used. "Besides, it's a great starter camera for a new person." Nisha finished getting details on the camera from Abhishek and thanked him. As she ended the call, I remember thinking how that did not seem right. I immediately called him back. For the rest of my life, I will always be glad that I did.

"Thank you for a great week, Bunty. It was so good to catch up and connect. I know it's not easy, but let's really make the effort to keep in touch."

"Yes, let's do that."

We said good-bye to each other and hung up.

That conversation had been around 9 am. Now it was 8 pm, and here was Jayshree on the phone.

"If somebody's heart stops beating for three hours, can they still be alive?"

What was she talking about? It made no sense. She was rambling and I could not understand what she was talking about. It was only at this point that the realisation dawned on me as she carried on talking.

"I am here in the hospital with Abhishek. I keep asking the doctors and nurses. No one is giving me a straight answer. And the police are here."

Oh . . . my . . . God.

The realisation of what she was saying finally hit me with such brutal force. How could this be true? That night, as I slept, I kept asking myself if I was in a bad dream. I woke on Tuesday morning and set off for work. My mind was in a daze. I couldn't concentrate. I came home early.

On Wednesday afternoon, a day later, I was in Kolkata standing at the gravestone of my friend. He was only thirty-two years of age.

When something like that happens to you, you truly understand you can never be the same again. It was a defining moment in my life!

Such a sudden loss like that is also a rude awakening as to how life can turn out not the way it should be. It defines life from then onwards. Once we have worked through our own grief and spent time with loved ones, who are also processing the same confused and heart-wrenching emotions, we are brought face-to-face with the realisation our life has to go on. You can't stop and step out of life. There are still jobs to be done, errands to be run, responsibilities to fulfil.

I had to ask myself a critical question:

Is the way I am living on a grand enough scale to handle the disappointments, disasters, and death that will certainly come again in the future?

And where do we go for the answers to such a question?

We have deep desires and intense longings. However, there is so much in our world that distracts us and leads us astray.

When such tragedies happen and the emotions are raw, the urgency and precarious reality of our life becomes tangible. We make resolutions and decisions; we have an inner urgency to live life with a sense of purpose and direction. But then it is easy, after a few weeks or months, for life to revert to its former state.

Where do we find the strength and courage to rise above the mediocre values and lack of meaning in contemporary life? Finding the answer to that question is the purpose of this book.

Since the death of my friend Bunty I have come to two important convictions about life. I have always had these convictions at some level but since his death in March 2014, these two convictions have become deeply embedded in me.

They don't only apply to me. I believe they apply to every human being who walks the earth.

1—Our life really matters

We are not simply meaningless atoms who came from nowhere and will end up nowhere. In the words of Shakespeare's Macbeth at a time of great despair, life is not simply ". . . a tale told by an idiot, full of sound and fury, signifying nothing".[15]

No day is ordinary. Every moment of every day matters, to be lived to the fullest extent possible.

If we live with a view to eternity, we will be proud of the legacy we are leaving to others. The suddenness of Bunty's death challenged me to consider the footprint we all leave in each other's lives. Bunty left a deep footprint on my life.

With so many ways that we get it wrong, along with all the distractions and complexities that confront us, we still have to live one day at a time. Some days may rush by in a blur and other days may drag, but we still have to live with sixty seconds in every minute, sixty minutes in every hour and twenty-four hours in every day. It is the same if you live in rural Africa or India, or work in a busy New York or London office.

My friend Kary Oberbrunner talks about 'redeeming the day'. It is an extension of the Latin *carpe diem,* which means, 'seize the day'.[16] While at times we can do well, we are continually looking to buy back value out of the time allotted to us.

2—We have to learn to walk in wisdom

> *The more you sweat in peace, the less you bleed in war.*
>
> —Chinese proverb

The Bible uses the analogy of a path, 700–800 times, comparing living life to walking along a pathway. Why is this metaphor so helpful?

Walking along a path, we progress by what seem to be steady, repeated and mundane actions. After all we are walking just one step at a time, one foot after the other! Then the same again. We could choose to run or even bounce forward with a series of handstands, Eventually, we are going to have to go back to reliable old walking—especially if the path stretches out for thousands of miles. And this path really can seem like thousands of miles. If we live for eighty years, our path has been 29,200 days! We can only live each one of those days one second at a time, with sixty of these seconds in a minute, sixty minutes every hour and twenty-four hours in every day. We can make plans and have ideas, but we do not know ultimately what lies ahead. What is guaranteed is that along with surprises and delights will be failures, frustrations, disappointments, despair and even death. Our Wisdom is what will give us the skills to handle whatever these eventualities are, and to handle them appropriately.

THE IMPLICATIONS OF THIS QUEST

But like any journey, we are moving towards a destination of some sort. Who we become, our final destination, is a product of how we do the little things every day, our little choices, our little attitudes, the basic disciplines, the things we spend our time doing every day. There is a place for the dramatic events. But it's the small, everyday decisions that set the trajectory of our life.

We instinctively realise this when somebody asks us how the last couple of weeks have been. We don't tell them about what we had for breakfast or that we brushed our teeth every day! That would be somewhat ridiculous. We are much more likely to talk about what we regard as the significant things that have happened.

Interestingly, the Bible sees it differently. The Bible is more concerned with how we are living day-to-day. When the Bible calls wisdom a pathway, when it talks about the way of wisdom, the path of wisdom, what it means is that we become wise by building on a set of daily practices. It means incorporating into our lives a certain set of daily disciplines, actions to do over and over and over. If you do them every day, over and over again, eventually you'll become a wise person. It is a very carefully thought through metaphor.

Acquiring wisdom is not like walking through a door for it to be given to you—game over. If it were a door, you would only have to be given the key, turn the latch, and, hey *presto*, wisdom would be yours. The day to day media in particular leads us to expect such an easy result in our modern lives; that success is guaranteed by following only very simple steps. The power of technology encourages us to expect a limited set of straightforward steps for a quick and easy solution.

This is not a new tendency. C. S. Lewis forsaw this many years ago when he wrote:

> *For the wise men of old the cardinal problem had been how to conform the soul to reality, and the solution had been knowledge, self-discipline, and virtue. For magic and applied science alike, the*

problem is how to subdue reality to the wishes of men: the solution is a technique.[17]

The point that C. S. Lewis makes is that wisdom, historically, has been seen as a long journey or quest over a significant stretch of time, requiring the repetition of simple things over a long period. Thus, wisdom is not like a tablet from the chemist that we take to arrive suddenly where we want to go. If you have seen *The Matrix* you will recognise this idea.

The idea of steady accumulation goes against the culture and mindset of our age. This almost instant gratification is part of the reason why the world we are living in is particularly complex and challenging. It has become increasingly so as moral structures and frameworks built by previous generations have been eroded and discarded.

I remember a vivid example of that from the early 1990s. I was just starting as a trainee psychiatrist. The woman booked to see me was one of the first patients with depression for whom I was responsible. At the time, I was a junior doctor on a six-month rotation gaining experience in a busy outpatient clinic. I had about twenty minutes to evaluate how she was doing, review her diagnosis and decide on treatment options. But this particular lady did not seem to be getting any better in spite of all the different medications and therapies that were being applied.

I went through her previous history and treatments, feeling something was not quite right. I must have been about the fourth or fifth junior doctor she had seen in the previous two years. One of the things we are taught in medical school is that when you feel stuck, go back and review the diagnosis for anything that might have been missed. I found myself saying to her, "Is there something that we are not aware of or are missing?"

This was an invitation to drop the bombshell.

"I have been having a prolonged affair with a neighbour who lives across the road. His wife does not know. In fact, she's my best friend. She's the friend who brought me to the clinic today. She's sitting outside the clinic room right now!"

I was one of the first people she had told. Her unresolved depression now made complete sense—she was living in guilt and out of congruency with herself. As sensitively as I could, I attempted to explain that no medication in the world could satisfactorily help her. To make progress, she would have to go through the difficult and painful task of facing up to what had happened. From there, she would have to deal with the future uncertain consequences of the decisions she had made. She did not need additional medication, a different kind of medication, or therapy. We could spend hours, days, weeks, months, years, or even decades going down those mistaken paths. But, now, she had a choice to make to turn back from the direction she had taken. As a psychiatrist, I could have kept on the path of adjusting the dose and type of her antidepressants. I could have added another antidepressant or more medication. But what I am convinced of was what she needed was wisdom. Her life experience and understanding of how life functions had hit a dead end. The only way out was to take a different turning and seek to live in wisdom with the choices she had made.

Maybe you have struggled with depression, stress, or burnout in your life—or maybe you haven't. Regardless of who you are and how great or little your successes may appear to be, I can guarantee there will be some unanswered questions in your life that are reaching out for greater wisdom.

One of the privileges in my life working as a psychiatrist and talking with a wide variety of people is that so many of those apparently successful people are, in my experience, actually quite insecure. They may appear to be all together and have the love and adoration of those around them. But behind all the success and accomplishments the world sees, there is surprisingly often a story of discontentment and personal insecurity. Some have called it 'The Imposter Syndrome'. All the fame and fortune in the world can mean nothing if you do not have the wisdom to go with it. These pithy verses from Proverbs challenge us to do everything we can to acquire wisdom:

The beginning of wisdom is this: Get wisdom. Though it cost all you have, get understanding. Cherish her, and she will exalt you; embrace her, and she will honour you. (Proverbs ch4 v7–8)

This fourth chapter of Proverbs keeps prodding and encouraging us to be single-minded and determined in acquiring wisdom, no matter the cost. Using the modern idea of a simple cost-benefit analysis, the reason is simple and clear. The results of not having wisdom can be devastating; we will make decisions that lead to a succession of difficulties and disasters. Avoiding those problems will need our full focus and attention.

The writer Tim Keller refers to verse 7:

> *[Wisdom] will lead to knowing God, knowing yourself, knowing the human heart and its ways, and knowing the times and seasons. And your decisions and choices will become wiser. We can paraphrase verse 7 like this: 'Here's how you get wisdom: Just get it!' Wisdom comes not to the most fortunate or intelligent but to those most determined to find it.*[18]
> (Proverbs ch 4 v7)

Wisdom comes not to the most highly qualified or most worthy, but to those who are most hungry to attain it. How hungry are you? Don't think you are not hungry. We are all hungry for something to fulfil and satisfy the empty and restless part of our hearts. But first, ask yourself, "Is what I am hungry for really going to provide the fulfilment, satisfaction and the contentment that I think that it will?"

We live in an age of technological advancement and opportunity way ahead of that in any previous generation. For increasing numbers of people, what would have seemed a fantasy or an impossibility even thirty years ago has now become commonplace.

Oscar Wilde said, "There are only two tragedies in life: one is not getting what one wants, and the other is getting it".[19]

Getting what we long for does not always provide the sense of completion or wholeness that we thought it would bring. There is still a sense of wanting more alongside the nagging thought that there must be more to life than this. For those fortunate enough to achieve their goals and dreams, lasting happiness may still be elusive. The initial euphoria and excitement is wonderful, but after a time the longing and yearning for more can come back with a sense of never seeming to be quite fulfilled. You may or may not have experienced something of that.

Time and attention is focused on making what we long for become a reality, thinking that this is what will bring happiness. A preoccupation with buying products or making money at the expense of health or personal relationships illustrates this well. Have you heard the witty, 'we buy things we don't need, with money we don't have, to impress people we don't even like!'?

Paradoxically, getting what we actually want could be the worst possible thing for us.

In *Counterfeit Gods,* Tim Keller tells of a woman he and his wife knew whose advancing age created in her a desperation to bear children.[20] Eventually, after much anguish and disappointment, she had two children of her own. The problem became that in her drive to give these precious children a perfect life, she was not able actually to enjoy them. She became overprotective, anxious and fearful to such an extent that her whole family became miserable. Her children's emotional suffering led the Kellers to fear that the very life that this mother was so desperate to give to her children would actually create irreparable distance between them and herself.

In the late 1980s the American writer Cynthia Heimel wrote, 'The minute a person becomes a celebrity is the same minute they become a monster.' Her article refers to the names of three well-known Hollywood stars she had known before they became famous. She describes them as being 'once perfectly pleasant human beings . . . now they have become supreme beings and their wrath is awful'.[21] Her conclusion is 'under the pressure of fame and celebrity, all our character flaws and miseries become twice as bad as they were before'.[22]

You may not be a mother with young children or a celebrity reading this book, but the same principle applies. If we have not done the necessary work on who we are, what we think will bring the longed for joy and satisfaction will instead crumble before us. We think that if it happened to us, we would be the exception. But there is a repeated historical cycle of those who seem to have it all actually being dissatisfied. It is a sobering reminder to question whether our hearts can ever be completely filled by what we think will bring ultimate fulfilment. Instead, these verses from the Book of Proverbs say that rather than yearn and long for what does not satisfy, let us instead hunger and thirst for wisdom!

> *The beginning of wisdom is this: Get wisdom. Though it cost all you have, get understanding. Cherish her, and she will exalt you; embrace her, and she will honour you.* (Proverbs ch 4 v7-8)

Some of that may seem a strange thing to say. To be honest, it doesn't seem all that comforting! Wisdom might cost us everything we have! But let us also consider the reward. The promise is that wisdom holds the key not only to all that we desire but also to rewards that are even better than we can imagine. Surely, this is seriously worth exploring!

The first step in getting wisdom is the realisation that we do not, at this point, have wisdom and that we do need it. As we think about that, let us reflect on our own life. What are the unanswered questions that still bother us or keep coming back? What are those areas of our life on which we have shut the door in frustration? What seems impossible to make sense of or understand? Those are the areas where we need wisdom! From a Biblical perspective, the heart is not the fount of our emotions but the source of our basic trusts and attitudes.

In the next chapter, we will reflect on why the world we live in is so much in need of wisdom. It is a world filled with information and of apparently never-ending and constant change. We need wisdom in order for our minds to begin to master it.

REVIEW QUESTIONS TO CONSIDER

1. Has the reality of death challenged the foundations of my life?
2. Do I see my life as a quest headed in a certain direction, or do I find myself becoming discouraged and distracted by a lack of meaning?
3. What do I look for that will bring ultimate joy and satisfaction in my life?
4. What pain am I hiding from myself, or from others, that prevents me from enjoying life?

2
WISDOM FOR THE MIND

The only person who likes change is a baby in wet diapers.

—Anonymous

Life can be difficult, and challenging. We are all able to know that on a theoretical or abstract level. It is only when a tragedy or difficult challenge arises that we begin to grasp the enormity of this reality.

The sudden loss of someone we deeply care about is heart-wrenching, as I experienced personally in March 2014. For a period, we re-evaluate almost everything about our lives. Where am I going? What am I doing? Why is life so short? Am I ready to die? What are my priorities? Are these priorities the right ones?

Have you felt deep pain and betrayal by someone who has hurt you or violated your trust? Do you wonder if you can ever trust anyone again? Are those experiences holding you back from making the most of your relationships in the present? How do you break free from this past?

Where do *we* go to for the answers to such questions? Where are the safe spaces for exploring answers? We all have deep desires and intense longings. However, there is so much that is distracting and leads us away from satisfying them. There are often feelings of being overwhelmed, of emptiness, being hurried, complexity and even absence of meaning.

Over the last few decades, the depth of the turmoil and confusion that creates these feelings has increased exponentially. The global uncertainty and confusion of the 2020 coronavirus pandemic is a prime example.

Let's look at two significant developments. In 2007, for the first time in the history of the world, there were more people living in cities than outside them.[23] In 2019, more than 50% of the global population had come online.[24] What are the implications?

Eric Teller, CEO of Google's Research and Development Laboratory, says that a thousand years ago a scientific or technological breakthrough would take a hundred years to make the world look or feel different.[25] Although what would be called the future had arrived, it was unevenly distributed around the world. Now that level of uneven distribution has rapidly diminished. By 1900, when there was a scientific or technological breakthrough, it would take twenty to thirty years for the world to look different. By the end of the second decade of the 21st century, with innovations such as mobile devices, broadband connectivity and cloud computing, the world could change in five to seven years. And this rate is continuing to speed up. Analysts predict that one of the next significant changes will be with the second half of the world's population, what is often called the developing world, also coming online. The coronavirus pandemic of 2020 has accelerated the pace of technological change. This rate of change is fast; it is becoming hard for us to keep up.

American physician and educator Richard Swenson describes this in terms of an exponentially rapid rate of change across numerous areas of our day-to-day lives.[26] The change in the last thirty years is such that if you compare it to all of human history, the rate of change for all the rest of our time on earth has been just a flat line. Our minds struggle to grasp, and to comprehend, this magnitude. To illustrate just how rapidly exponential numbers accumulate, think of the following simple exercise. If you fold a piece of paper in half forty-five times, how thick do you think it would be? The staggering answer is that it would be thick enough to reach from here to the moon.[27]

Ray Kurzweil (Director of Engineering at Google) builds on this by saying that the next 100 years will be equivalent, at the present rate of change, to the last 20,000 years of progress.[28] In the world of business, we are already seeing some incredible examples of completely new types of business. Take the global accommodation app Airbnb. At the time of this writing, Airbnb is the world's largest renter of accommodation. It offers and transacts more rooms than all of the biggest hotel groups combined. Airbnb is currently valued at $31 billion, which is twice the value of the Hilton group founded in 1919. It is run with only 1% of the number of Hilton employees, has been in existence since only 2008, and the company does not own a single room! Or look at Uber, the world's largest taxi company. Since being created in 2009, Uber has grown to a valuation of $70 billion without owning a single car.[29]

At the level of both society and ourselves there are unprecedented changes. Political, social and environmental forces are changing the structures and norms of everyday life, radically. Around the world there are diminishing numbers of people actively engaged in work. Dissatisfaction with these changes is growing worldwide. This unrest is having serious global economic effects along with the emotional, psychological and spiritual costs to our souls and society at large. And that is quite separate from the economic impact of the 2020 global pandemic.

It is estimated that 264 million people around the world suffer from depression, which is the leading cause of disability and a major contributor to ill-health.[30] In the Western world, suicide rates continue to rise. Our priorities, which are a frequent root of this depression, continue to be irrational and illogical. We, as the human race, spend each year on ice cream ($59 billion) more than double what is spent on providing "the basic human dignities of education, health care and sanitation for all humans on earth".[31] In addition to this failure to provide is the active onslaught of violence, war, inequality, injustice, pollution, corruption and systemic racism of which we are made very aware through mainstream media on a daily basis. But those feelings of uncertainty, constant change and of confusion have always been with us.

To understand this more, we need to go to the world of quantum mechanics. For centuries, the world has been understood in terms of what has been called determinism or a clockwork universe. What that means is all the components of a system are easily measurable and predictable. One lever or cog in a machine affects another cog or lever, so the results and consequences can be controlled and managed in a consistent way. Often it is like this. But since the 20th century, quantum physics has completely revolutionised our understanding of how the universe works. It is this understanding that underlies, for example, the amazing things we can do with our smartphones and mobile technology. However, this understanding has not been adopted in the same way by popular culture, which continues to see the world as deterministic and functioning like clockwork.

In 1932, Werner Heisenberg, a German physicist, won the Nobel prize for his theory of quantum mechanics. His development of what became known as Heisenberg's Uncertainty Principle has had profound consequences on our understanding of the universe. This principle states that we cannot know both the precise position and the momentum of a quantum particle at the same time. Sometimes matter behaves like a particle by appearing to be in one place at one time, and sometimes (this is where it gets mind-blowing) it behaves like a wave by appearing to be in several places at the same time. A helpful analogy is to think of a wave that can spread itself out over a whole pond. This is known as the duality of nature and is explained as 'the imprecise measurement of initial conditions precludes the precise prediction of future outcomes'.[32] To put it more simply, there will always be an element of uncertainty—life is infinitely uncertain.

Uncertainty has always existed.[33] There is a word that encapsulates this. It has roots in military terminology, but is being increasingly used to describe the complex and challenging world of our daily lives. Largely due to the exponential increase in microchip technology, we are living through levels of change and disruption which were previously unimaginable. It is claimed that more information has been produced in the last 30 years than in all the previous 5,000 years combined. This change is not slowing down.[34]

Before we look at that word which describes how our world is changing, let's put things in context. Here is how the late Peter Drucker, one of the greatest management teachers of the 20th century, describes the modern world: 'We are in one of those great historical periods that occur every 200–300 years when people do not understand the world anymore and the past is not sufficient to explain the future'.[35]

For a long time it may not have felt like that. Particularly for those in power and those relatively well off, the world has been comparatively safe and predictable. That has certainly been the case for those of us in the affluent countries of the West.

Those of us enjoying Western-style civilisation and culture today have a greater need of wisdom than ever before. We have more choices about life than anyone who has come before us. That applies to both the big choices and to the moment-by-moment daily choices.

In the past, traditional cultures made your mind up for you about the big choices. In these cultures, like that of my parents, somebody else chose your wife or your husband. The family or society told you what you had to do, what your job would be when you grew up, what town you were going to live in and who your friends would be. If you tried to move to another town, the local people would ask, "What are you doing over here? Your family is from that other town. Get back there. You don't belong here. Go back to where you came from". There were few options, and it was not possible to attempt anything radically different.

Smaller but no less significant day-to-day choices fared no better. Decisions about how we spent our own time were very limited.

How those times have changed! There is no limit to the direction our lives may take. We face an explosion of choices and options. Everything is wide open. Often we are perplexed when faced by a choice between two alternatives, and lack the wisdom to decide. It is much harder when these options are ten, or a hundred, or more.

How do we describe this new world?

The acronym VUCA helps—the world is

Volatile, Uncertain, Complex and Ambiguous.

This is the military term which I mentioned earlier. The theory behind VUCA developed from US military thinking in the period after the Cold War and has now been widely adopted.

Here is what these terms mean, with some striking examples.

Volatile. The size and speed of change is continually increasing. New companies become billion-dollar organisations in only a few years. What were once long-established institutions become obsolete, rapidly disappearing. The former include Facebook and WhatsApp; the latter makes us think of companies like Kodak.

From its launch in 2004 in a college dormitory, Facebook grew from zero to over 1.4 billion users in a little over ten years. By 2020 this had almost doubled to 2.4 billion users. WhatsApp is similar, starting in 2009 and now being the most popular messaging app in the world, with over 2 billion current users. When it was bought by Facebook in 2014 for $16 billion, there were only fifty-five employees[36]

Kodak is a complete contrast. The company was started in 1884 with the invention of photographic film. For a century Kodak was synonymous with photography. They created the world's first digital camera in 1995. A year later, Kodak had a 90% market share for photographic film and an 85% share of camera sales in the United States. They reached their peak of 145,000 employees in the late 1980s. Kodak dominated the market and was secure. What could possibly go wrong? In reality, a good deal. They were unable to keep up with the relentless technological change in the photography industry. In 2012 Kodak filed for bankruptcy and closed down. They were destroyed by the digital technology they had themselves invented![37]

Uncertain. What we have learnt from past experience is less and less relevant in explaining what the future will be. That is not new. It implies that increasingly often, whatever our level of expertise, we do not really know what the future holds. To illustrate this, what do these predictions from experts in the past say about predicting the future:

'The phonograph is of no commercial value.' Thomas Edison said this, remarking on his own invention in 1880.[38] (In case you are wondering, the phonograph was the very first invention to record sound. From the phonograph came records, cassettes, CD players and eventually digital music.)

'There is no likelihood man can ever tap the power of the atom.' Robert Millikan, Nobel Prize winner in physics, 1920.[39]

'It is an idle dream to imagine that automobiles will take the place of railways in the long-distance movement of passengers.' Third American Road Congress, 1913.[40]

'I think there is a world market for about five computers.' Thomas Watson, IBM's chairman, said this in 1943.[41]

'There is no reason for any individual to have a computer in his home.' Ken Olsen, president of big business mainframe computer manufacturer Digital Equipment Corporation, who was arguing against the personal computer in 1977.[42]

'So we went to Atari and said, "Hey we've got this amazing thing, even built with some of your parts, and what do you think about funding us? Or we'll give it to you. We just want to do it. Pay our salary, we'll come work for you". And they said, "No". So then we went to Hewlett-Packard and they said, "Hey, we don't need you. You haven't got through college yet."'[43] Steve Jobs, founder of Apple Computer Inc., talking about attempts by himself and Steve Wozniak to distribute their personal computer.

'We don't like their sound, and guitar music is on the way out.'[44] Decca Records said this when they rejected the Beatles in 1962.

'The abdomen, the chest and the brain will forever be shut from the intrusion of the wise and humane surgeon.'[45] John Eric Erickson, British surgeon who was appointed Surgeon Extraordinary to Queen Victoria in 1873.

'The abolishment of pain in surgery is a chimera. It is absurd to go on seeking it . . . knife and pain are two words in surgery that must forever be associated with the consciousness of the patient.'[46] Dr Alfred Velpeau, a French surgeon, in 1839.

'No one will pay good money to get from Berlin to Potsdam in one hour when he can ride his horse there in one day for free.'[47] King William I of Prussia, in 1864, on first hearing about the invention of trains.

'So many centuries after the Creation, it is unlikely that anyone could find hitherto unknown lands of any value.' A committee advising King Ferdinand and Queen Isabella of Spain regarding a proposal they received from Christopher Columbus in 1486.[48]

Reading such confident pronouncements by experts in their fields at the time does make me wonder how much of what is confidently pronounced by experts today is equally way off about our future. Time will also tell about the predictions I quoted at the beginning of this chapter! As the American baseball legend and creator of Berra-isms, Yogi Berra, quipped, 'It is tough to make predictions, especially about the future!'

Often, it's the smartest people who can think of all the reasons why something is not possible. In some ways, they are right. All their learning and education proves to them why something cannot happen. However, there are perspectives and changes outside their viewpoint they could never have imagined or predicted. There is so little we can confidently know about the future—and today, that holds even more true.

Complexity. All aspects of life are interrelated in ways that are beyond what we have thought or even imagined. The power of the microchip and unprecedented advances in communication empower events on the other side of the world to have an almost immediate impact on us. And vice versa. We can know about events instantaneously. But the availability of such information way exceeds the pace at which we can make sense of and interpret it. Technological advances have overtaken our level of wisdom to comprehend them.

Ambiguous. There is a lack of clarity about what events mean and what effect they may have. It is becoming increasingly challenging to make a quick decision about whether an event is of great importance or is only a trivial distraction. With a large amount of information coming from several different directions, it is increasingly difficult to prioritise what is important and what is not.

I recall an email I received at work a few years ago. It first appeared to be a trivial matter relating to a course I had attended five years earlier. An issue which appeared to be of no consequence led eventually to six months of paperwork and intense activity before it was resolved. That ambiguity caused significant stress before it was clarified and could be dealt with properly. The issue was unrelated to technical expertise or competence. Rather, it was an exercise in bureaucracy that diverted scarce time and energy from more important matters.

At the societal level in the West we see this with the huge ambiguity around engagement with present-day sexuality and gender classification. For millennia, societies and cultures around the world have generally functioned with two genders and an understanding of heterosexual union as the normal acceptable practice. Now increasingly strident voices claim a choice of as many as sixty-four terms to describe gender identity and sexual preference. In addition, some universities advocate as many as thirty words for addressing people using pronouns other than the simple male or female equivalent. To question this can invite strong hostility and anger from some quarters.

A 'VUCA' world like this presents challenges that previously were never imagined. Albert Einstein said, 'The significant problems we face cannot be solved at the same level of thinking we were at when we created them'.[49] If we insist on doing what we have always done, then we will achieve the same results we have always achieved. It is worth remembering the remark that 'repeating the same thing and expecting a different result is a definition of insanity!' To change the results in our lives, we have to do different things. And to do different things requires us to think differently. To deal with these challenges, new paradigms of thinking and action are going to have to emerge. But let us be grateful that with great challenges also come unprecedented opportunities.

Through their lives and work, both Peter Drucker and songwriter Bob Dylan have brought to our attention changes in the last few decades. Change has always been a part of human existence. Several millenia ago the Old Testament book Ecclesiastes said,

There's an opportune time to do things, a right time for everything on the earth:

A right time for birth and another for death,
A right time to plant and another to reap,
A right time to kill and another to heal,
A right time to destroy and another to construct,
A right time to cry and another to laugh,
A right time to lament and another to cheer,
A right time to make love and another to abstain,

A right time to embrace and another to part,
A right time to search and another to count your losses,
A right time to hold on and another to let go,
A right time to rip out and another to mend,
A right time to shut up and another to speak up,
A right time to love and another to hate,
A right time to wage war and another to make peace.
(Ecclesiastes ch 3 v1–8, The Message translation)

I have always been thrilled by the poetic rhythm of these lines. They seem so contemporary that one can imagine Bob Dylan writing them.

More than 3,000 years later with the barely credible range of choices offered in our VUCA world, we need great and lasting wisdom to discern the right courses of action.

The misguided forecasts which I gave above are characteristic of the pitfalls in a VUCA world. They heighten the particular need for wisdom now, in this day and age.

Technology and the digital age surround us with information—more accurately, we're drowning in information. This applies across all subjects. The rule of thumb is that the amount of information on any subject doubles every eighteen months, in some sectors sooner. Reuters claim that the amount of information produced in the last thirty years is more than the previous 5,000 years combined.[50] The famous quote from former Google CEO, Eric Schmidt, is that, "There were 5 exabytes of information created between the dawn of civilization through to 2003, but that much information is now created every 2 days".[51] There is a huge amount of information out there; but this information is not the same as wisdom. Mere possession or access to information is not sufficient to navigate the complexities of life.

This explosion of information underlies the almost impossible variety from which we feel a responsibility to make the right choice. Exponential increase in an already overwhelming range of options has a dramatic impact on lives which are often already over-stretched.

Back in the 1990s Peter Drucker predicted this decision fatigue when he wrote,

> *In a few hundred years, when the history of our time is written from a long-term perspective, it is likely that the most important event those historians will see is not technology, not the Internet, not e-commerce. It is the unprecedented change in the human condition. For the first time—literally—substantial and rapidly growing numbers of people have choices. For the first time, they will have to manage themselves. And society is totally unprepared for it.*[52]

Peter Drucker's foresight over thirty years ago has been proven correct. We have, as a society, been totally unprepared for this dramatic shift, particularly those living in the industrialised world. He is saying that the biggest change in modern society is the creeping increase of choices. Those choices range from which cereal I have to start the morning (Wikipedia records over 500 cereals to choose from in the Western world) to how I choose to spend my time during the rest of the day.

This choice increased gradually, with us hardly being aware. It is now layering stress and complexity onto already congested lives. Over thirty to forty years a staggering increase has developed in the variety of foods and products that we can buy from our supermarkets. Yet, we know from experience that we need only a fraction of this for our day-to-day needs.

The frog in a pot of gradually heating water didn't notice the increasing warmth until it was too late. Similarly, we have failed to notice the increasing choice that is now threatening us. The average person in the Western world has to make as many as an estimated 35,000 decisions every day![53] The water in our pot is beginning to boil!

Why does this matter? It matters because our brains struggle to tell the difference between a small decision and a major one.

We expend energy making a choice, regardless of importance. Unless we have respite, the quality of our decisions deteriorates over time. Just as our muscles fatigue from an excess of exercise, so do our minds fatigue from an excess of decision-making.

This is not surprising. The root of the word *decide* is to 'cut off' or 'kill off'.[54] It is the same root as for the word 'homicide' (to murder). With so many choices, there is fear that by making one choice, we are missing out on a better option. We have even developed a new word for it—FOMO or The Fear of Missing Out! The result is described as 'analysis paralysis', meaning that we have so many choices that we make no decision at all. There are only a finite number of decisions we can make each day before suffering from decision-fatigue.

Stress, fatigue and our emotions all affect us. A fascinating Israeli research study from Ben-Gurion University of the Negev illustrates this. It looked at the results of 1,112 parole board hearings in Israeli prisons over a ten-month period. The results were striking. They showed that the odds that prisoners would be successfully paroled started off fairly high at around 65% and quickly plummet to zero over the course of a few hours. After the judges returned from their break, the odds climbed straight back up to 65% before resuming their downward slide. A prisoner's fate hinges upon the point in the day that their case is heard.[55,56] A decision that should be based on objective facts is, instead, prone to the idiosyncrasies of tired individuals.

Decision fatigue is something that really exists for all of us. We all have a finite limit to the number of decisions we can make each day—after a certain point we simply lapse into shut-down mode.

The result is that some of the most successful people automate what they consider insignificant decisions so they can invest their limited attention on the bigger decisions. By reducing their daily decisions, they are able to exert greater focus and energy on the ones they deem most important.

A good example is that extremely busy leaders like Steve Jobs, Mark Zuckerberg and Barack Obama simplify life by pre-deciding their wardrobe. That might seem relatively trivial. Yet, by dealing with the trivial beforehand, space is created for more important matters.

DISAPPOINTMENT

What is the impact of constant decisionmaking on our relationships, our emotions and our mental wellbeing? There is one word—disappointment. A sense of general dissatisfaction with life, thinking that something better must be around the corner.

Being forewarned is being forearmed. Disappointment is an experience we all go through at some time in our lives. While it is a form of suffering, it is not as acute, dramatic, heart-wrenching and extremely painful as sudden bereavement, irreparably broken relationships, betrayal, torture, or persecution.

Disappointment is subtler and more insidious. But it can be just as challenging. Like a cancer hidden beneath the surface, it can eat away and destroy our sense of joy or well-being. It is often linked with the general sense of frustration that leads to depression, anger, cynicism, or bitterness.

Disappointment can be a product of affluence, with an abundance of choices and opportunities. (If you can afford to buy this book or are reading this on a computer or smartphone, then that includes you!) Our reality is that we have privileges and possibilities that are beyond the wildest imaginations of previous generations. But it doesn't feel like that. We are inclined to something along the lines of 'Yes, I should be thankful, but. . . .' What we say to ourself or others after the word 'but' defines the disappointment we're talking about.

The English pastor John Hindley, in *Dealing with Disappointment: How to Find Joy When Life Doesn't Feel Great*, defines disappointment as 'what we experience when we expect satisfaction and this satisfaction is denied'.[57] He gives the banal, but very recognisable, example of coming home from a long day's work expecting his family to welcome him, only to find they are out somewhere else. So, he feels disappointed—he expected a certain satisfaction, and it was denied. There is nothing earth-shattering about that feeling, but it is a seed of potential future feelings and actions.

Disappointment is the sense of feeling empty and dissatisfied even though life seems successful; our marriage is OK, family life is OK and we have achieved our dreams.

I remember how acutely I felt that in the summer of 2001. I had just been confirmed as a consultant psychiatrist. After earning a six-year medical degree and doing eleven years of postgraduate work, I had reached what many recognise as the top of the career ladder. Happily married, my wife and I had joyfully welcomed the arrival of our third child a few months earlier. I was actively involved in church leadership and ministry. On the surface, everything seemed good and I had a lot to be thankful for. But (there *was* a but) the biggest thing I remember feeling at that time was a profound sense of emptiness. It was deeply disappointing. All those things which I had thought would fill and complete me didn't seem quite enough.

It is very hard to talk to others about this disappointment, yet I am convinced it is an increasingly common experience. Although in so many ways we have never had it so good, there is a widespread and profound sense that something vital is missing.

There are three main dangers of unchecked disappointment: despair and a general sense of hopelessness, escapism and a loss of perspective

1—Despair and a general sense of hopelessness

Henry David Thoreau, the author of *Walden*, wrote about how many people 'live lives of quiet desperation and go to their graves with the song still in them'.[58] This is the chronic long-term view of disappointment; as we get older, we give up on our dreams and ambitions, settling for a life of resignation and cynicism about almost everything. In a more acute form, this can follow success and achievement of all that we have ever wanted. Jonny Wilkinson, the rugby player who scored the winning drop goal in 2003 to dramatically give England the World Cup Trophy, suddenly found a great emptiness behind the euphoria and celebration.

He wrote in his autobiography, *Tackling Life*, 'Within hours of that last kick I was tumbling out of control . . . I am only as good as my last kick . . . I was afflicted with a powerful fear of failure and did not know how to free myself from it. The better things were, the more I had to lose'.[59] This loss of hope is such a private experience that we rarely hear people talk openly about it.

2—Escapism

When we engage in escapism, we centre our life around superficialities where the most exciting things happening are television, Netflix binges, drink, or the next holiday. There is nothing inherently wrong with these activities; the danger develops when they are all that our life centres around. We risk escaping into a separate identity, or an alter-ego. Rather than face the reality of our current situation, we escape into a fantasy world. The core focus shifts to our desires and wants. Classically this can progress to pornography addiction or sliding into an adulterous affair.

With the intense longings that are sometimes aroused in our heart, it is easy to succumb to self-centred desires and aspirations. The advertising industry and marketeers know that well. The devastating impact on the lives of individuals and families of the pornography industry is a prime example. Internet analytics show that sex is the number one search topic, comprising 25% of total search requests. Something like 40% of those addicted to pornography lose their spouse, 58% suffer significant financial loss and a third lose their job.[60] Pornography increases the rate of marital infidelity by more than 300%.[61] Severe clinical depression is reported twice as frequently among internet pornography users compared to non-users.[62] Such tragedy does not happen overnight but is the culmination of a series of linked private decisions over time.

For all that, such extreme outcomes are not inevitable. We can live for those short moments of happiness while running the rest of life at a steady plod. We achieve this through booking our next holiday the moment we get home from the last one. We find ourselves constantly talking about holidays, putting up photos everywhere and living our lives through those two, three or four weeks of the year. The rest of life is just filling in time, doing what must be done to get back to the beach or the ski slopes. Entertainment is also a great means of escaping the apparent boredom of our lives. The next episode on Netflix becomes the only exciting part of life. The purpose of our day is to struggle through the nine-to-five routine of work, get the children to bed and then watch the programme we have been anticipating all day. As John Hindley puts it, 'The highlight of my weekend easily becomes the film I saw on Saturday night and not the Jesus I saw on Sunday night'.[63]

What we escape to in our thoughts is a good indication of what we truly worship.

We will be exploring this later on.

3—Loss of perspective

When we lose perspective, we run the risk of losing the big picture of who we are and what our life is ultimately about. We become centred on ourself and how we are feeling to the exclusion of everyone and everything else. Life becomes all about only ourselves, with no greater or deeper story than our personal wants and desires. If we stand on the beach staring at a pebble in our hand, we lose sight of the vast ocean in front of us. If disappointment is all that we can see, we fail to see and appreciate everything that is positive in our lives.

From disappointment, it is easy to slip into one of the next stages—loneliness, worry and anxiety, stress, burnout and depression.

Finally, disappointment twists into cynicism. In reality, cynicism is a self-defence mechanism. It's hard for our hopes to be dashed if we had never allowed them to rise high to begin with. Sadly, that kind of cynicism poisons our soul. The great danger is that it can sabotage all the good things in our lives.

The challenging complexity of this world does place a heavy toll on us. You may recall Thoreau's comment quoted earlier, 'Most people live lives of quiet desperation and die with their song still inside of them'. The optimistic possibility which he lays before us is less well known. 'They honestly think there is no choice left. But alert and healthy natures remember that the sun rose clear. It is never too late to give up our prejudices'.[64] If we find and access a wisdom for our lives, it will both satisfy our minds and capture the heart of our trusts and attitudes.

REVIEW QUESTIONS TO CONSIDER

1. How much have I been personally impacted and unsettled by the rapid changes in the world of which we are a part?
2. How do I handle the explosion of choices that are now available to me?
3. How much has disappointment shaped my life?
4. Where do I go to escape from disappointment and harshness in life?

3
WISDOM FOR LIFE

What lies behind us and what lies before us are tiny matters compared to what lies within us.

—Henry Stanley Haskins

Along with good and joy there is pain and there are problems. It is important to acknowledge how much of that pain extends to our own lives. This chapter covers some uncomfortable topics. But, in order to meet new challenges, we are going to have to understand what are the obstacles that inhibit growth in our lives. Genuine growth springs from lessons learnt enduring hardships thrust upon us in life.

In order to understand how to move forward, it is helpful to understand where we have been and how we arrived there. It is often uncomfortable doing the spade work to get there. However, the more we understand the problems of lacking wisdom, the greater will be our motivation to change the direction of our lives and ensure that we do develop wisdom.

As we saw in the last chapter, the rate of change in our lives has been developing exponentially in recent times. The result is that we are the most over-informed but under-reflective civilisation in human history. What are some of the consequences of that?

Let's explore these consequences on an individual level, in our relations with others and then for society in general. The first few consequences may seem relatively trivial and even minor but they are the foundations of greater and deeper issues.

This list is by no means exhaustive. But as many of these examples are my own or come from people with whom I have spoken, they have particular relevance.

DISCONTENTMENT

We have never had life so good. The opportunities and resources available to us were unheard of even a few decades ago. But along with them has come a sense of entitlement and of rarely feeling convincingly satisfied. We discovered earlier how we even have a word for it—FOMO or the Fear Of Missing Out! Through social media, we compare ourselves with the lives of many others. We find ourselves trying to impress people we don't really like by doing and buying things we don't really want or need, often with money we don't even have! And we fall into the belief that many other people are living happier and more exciting lives than our own. When we feel miserable and inadequate, which is easy when we compare our internal lives with the apparent success and positivity of someone else's external life, we forget that what we see on social media is carefully curated with selected photos and polished write-ups.

Matters are made worse when what we thought would make us happy does not live up to our exciting initial expectations. I still remember the euphoria I felt the first time I received an email! I sent my own to a friend late one evening in the late 1990s and the next morning, I received a reply! Now, when I open my inbox there are usually a mixed range of emotions—none of which are euphoria! Technology has made great promises to us about bringing ease and simplicity to our lives. In some ways, it has indeed provided us with just this. At the same time we find ourselves distanced from fulfilment, still not satisfied. Technology's great advances do not answer the discontentment of restless hearts. There are deeper issues at our core that require addressing.

FEAR AND DREAD

Fear is a universal human experience. At high-levels it creates panic or terror, at a low level we might call it concern or sometimes nervousness. By contrast, dread is less specific than fear; it is an attitude that something is sure to go wrong, if it has not already done so.

All of us are prone to being frightened and scared. What appears to have changed more recently is the sheer quantity of what can overwhelm and disturb us. News channels and other media produce a steady stream of negative attitudes and reporting which induces fear. There is something fascinating about bad news, tragedies and disasters that encourages us to find out more. We become submerged in a negative outlook. The impact of information technology invading all aspects of our lives makes it easy to become absorbed and fixated on the negative aspects without the relief of perspective or balance. Unless we are careful, this inbalance leads to a sense of dread and foreboding.

It's one thing to be shy and introverted, but it's another to be isolated and incapable of interacting with other people. What we fear controls us; the fear that we face up to we can control. Overcoming fears and challenges is basic to growing. Finding this growth means intentionally going outside our comfort zone—everything we truly long for lies beyond where we feel comfortable.

SHAME

We struggle with and do not talk enough about shame. Shame is universal and one of the most primitive emotions we experience. The only people who don't experience shame lack the capacity for empathy and human connection. We have a choice between an admission of experiencing shame or facing up to the development of what psychiatrists would describe as sociopathic tendencies!

American sociology professor and author Brené Brown describes factors surrounding shame. She explains that while shame is a universal experience, it is also something we are all afraid to talk about. Unfortunately, the less we feel able to talk about shame, the more it takes a hold on our lives.[65]

The twelve shame categories that Brené Brown has identified are appearance and body image, money and work, motherhood/fatherhood, family, parenting, mental and physical health, addiction, sex, ageing, religion, surviving trauma and being stereotyped and labelled.[66] All of these are able to create a deeply private feeling of fear about not being good enough, which can come to dominate our thinking.

During Brené Brown's research, participants revealed shame right across their lives:

> Shame is getting laid off and having to tell my pregnant wife.
> Shame is having someone ask me, 'When are you due?' when I am not pregnant.
> Shame is hiding the fact I am in recovery.
> Shame is raging at my kids.
> Shame is my boss calling me an idiot in front of the client.
> Shame is not making partner in your place of employment.
> Shame is my husband leaving me for my next-door neighbour.
> Shame is my wife asking for a divorce, and telling me she wants children but not with me.
> Shame is my DUI (driving under the influence of alcohol).
> Shame is infertility.
> Shame is telling my fiancé that my dad lives in France when in fact he is in prison.
> Shame is Internet porn.
> Shame is flunking out of school. Twice.
> Shame is hearing through the walls my parents fight and wondering if I am the only one who feels this afraid.[67]

As raw and uncomfortable as these examples are, there is a pathway through these paralysing and all-consuming emotions.

Brown calls this pathway stress resilience; the result is empathy and healing.

WORRY AND ANXIETY

We live in what has been called an Age of Anxiety. There is something about life (maybe it has always been there) that suggests everything is actually fragile. A constant barrage of information and data coming from all directions suggests that major problems and catastrophes are lurking around the corner. There is no shortage of subjects to worry about—global warming, viral pandemics, threats of rogue states like North Korea developing nuclear weapons, or the risk of terrorist attacks to name only a few.

I remember the very personal experience of walking to school in 1980 and hearing that Ronald Regan had been elected president of the United States. The news was full of speculation that within a few years we would have nuclear war with what was then known as the Soviet Union. The United Kingdom government had even commissioned public information programmes on what to do in case of nuclear fallout! I can still vividly remember that walk to school as a fifteen-year-old boy thinking, *What is the point of me studying anything when it seems practically inevitable we will all die from a nuclear attack?* As a teenager, I didn't have much of a positive outlook on life! That experience was not confined to me alone. All these years later, I see increasing numbers of people experience life this way, living with anxiety.

LONELINESS

In many ways, life has never been so easy. We are able to connect practically instantaneously with anyone around the world. A major event happens on the other side of the planet and almost immediately we know about it. We can see and connect with family and friends anywhere on the planet, literally at the click of a button. Yet with all this connectivity we can at the same time feel deeply lonely.

Loneliness is such a factor of modern life in much of our world that campaigns to reduce it have been launched in Britain, Denmark and Australia. In Japan, the government has surveyed *hikikomori*, or 'people who shut themselves in their homes'. Vivek Murthy, a former surgeon-general of the United States, called loneliness an epidemic whose impact on health he likened to obesity or smoking fifteen cigarettes per day. In January 2018, the British government went as far as appointing a Minister for Loneliness.[68]

Loneliness is not the same as social isolation, which is defined as how often a person meets or speaks to friends and family. It's also different from solitude, which is more of a choice to be alone.

The key to understanding loneliness is its definition as perceived social isolation, the feeling of not having the social connection and contacts one would like. Someone who appears to be more isolated than the average person is also more likely to be lonely, but it's also possible to feel lonely when you are surrounded by plenty of other people. I recall growing up in the United Kingdom and feeling lonely and disconnected from my South Asian family and culture in India. That created another problem: when I went to my extended family in India, I quickly felt lonely and homesick for the connections and comforts of England!

What do we actually mean by loneliness?

Researchers define loneliness as a perception of social isolation, a feeling of lacking the social contacts one wants. Of course, those who are physically isolated are much more likely than the average person to feel lonely. But loneliness can also strike those with seemingly ample friends and family living in seemingly healthy relationships. The mere fact of being on one's own is not always a bad thing and learning to live with solitude can be incredibly enriching and rewarding (more on that later). It is loneliness which is harmful.

In 2018, *The Economist* and the Kaiser Family Foundation (KFF), an American non-profit group focused on health, surveyed representative samples of people in three rich countries. The study found that 9% of adults in Japan, 22% in America and 23% in Britain 'always or often feel lonely, lack companionship, or feel left out or isolated'.[69]

It is only relatively recently that the links between relationships and health have been studied. In 2015, a meta-analysis led by Julianne Holt-Lunstad of Brigham Young University in Utah synthesised seventy papers through which 3.4 million participants were followed over an average of seven years. She found that after accounting for differences in age and health status, those classified as lonely had a 26% higher risk of dying and those living alone had a 32% higher probability.[70]

Smaller-scale studies have found correlations between loneliness and isolation and a range of health problems, including heart attacks, strokes, cancers, eating disorders, drug abuse, sleep deprivation, depression, alcoholism and anxiety. Some research suggests that the lonely are more likely to suffer from cognitive decline and a quicker progression of Alzheimer's disease.

STRESS

Talking about stress and its consequences is a very common feature of modern life. Practically everyone we come across talks about how they are struggling to do more with less or the toll that workload pressure is having on them. We can find ourselves waking up in the morning saying 'I need more sleep' and going to bed at night thinking 'I didn't get enough done today'.

The impact of stress includes:

- a significant link to all the leading causes of death, such as cardiovascular disease, cancer, accidents and suicide
- a very high proportion of visits to primary health care providers (GPs)
- up to 40% of all work-related illnesses in the United Kingdom

- heart attacks occurring on a Monday morning after the weekend more than at any other time of the week[71,72]

But what do we mean by stress? Why is it important and what can be done about it?

The word 'stress' is often used in both a confusing and ambiguous way. The reason that it is confusing is that 'stress' can refer to a wide range of mental, physical and social ill health at home or at work. It can also be ambiguous by refering either to an external stimulus acting on the individual or how an individual reacts to that stimulus. (More on that later.)

A possible explanation of why we are confused with the word 'stress' is because it comes from the world of physics, where it originally defined the intensity of a force per unit area. The word is derived from the Latin word *stringere,* which means 'to draw tight'.[73] This origin matches the idea that human stress arises from an imbalance between demands and resources.

In 1936, Hans Selye, an Austro-Hungarian endocrinologist and Noble prize winner, proposed three stages of the Stress Response: alarm, adaptation and eventual exhaustion. After he retired, Hans Selye apologised for a serious mistake with his stress research. He confessed that stress was the wrong term and that he should have described his research findings as the strain syndrome. His explanation was that use of the word stress created the perception that it's something that happens to us and is continually acting on us. He emphasised the importance of a distinction between the external pressure (stress) and the internal effect (strain).[74]

Our response to the external pressure, the stress, is at least as important as what is happening inside us, the strain. This is a profound observation which opens the door to gaining effective control of the different pressures we face in life.

The impact of these pressures is highlighted by our mind's reaction to negativity. The first thing our brain does is to turn off ten to twenty IQ points. This is a natural physiological reaction of our brain being designed to help us survive threatening attacks, generally from predators. Unchecked, this response has profound consequences.

Kelly McGonigal has thought about this in great detail. She is a Stanford University health psychologist who seeks to translate academic research into practical strategies for developing health, happiness and personal success. Her short fourteen-minute TED Talk illustrates the power of how our thinking about stress dramatically affects our overall health and well-being.[75]

Her talk is based on three observations.

The first starts with a 2012 study that tracked 30,000 adults in the United States for eight years. The study was based on two simple questions:

- *How much stress have you experienced in the last year?*
- *Do you believe stress is harmful for your health?*

What is fascinating is that those who experienced a lot of stress in the previous year had a 43% increased risk of dying, but that was only true for those who also believed stress is harmful for your health. What is more, those who experienced a lot of stress but did not view stress as harmful were no more likely to die. They actually had the lowest risk of dying of anyone in the study, including those who had relatively little stress.

The staggering conclusion was that over the eight years the study was conducted, 182,000 Americans died not from stress but from simply believing stress is bad for you. McGonigal's extrapolation is that simply believing stress is bad for you was, in 2012, the 15th largest cause of death in the United States, killing more people than skin cancer, HIV/AIDS and homicide.

What can we can conclude from these results? That when we change our thinking about stress, we can change our body's response to stress.

Typically, when we are having a stress response, our heart rate goes up and our blood vessels constrict. The key is how we interpret those physiological symptoms. When someone views their stress response as helpful, their cardiovascular profile resembles what happens in moments of joy and courage.

According to McGonigal, 'Over a lifetime of stressful experiences, this one biological change could be the difference between a stress-induced heart attack at age fifty and living well into your nineties. And this is what the new science of stress reveals—how you think about stress matters'.

BURNOUT

Looking back, I have burnt out at least three times in my life. The first two episodes occurred at the end of my first and third years of studying medicine at university. The combined challenges of moving away from home, feeling out of my depth academically and being isolated and alone gradually took their toll.

The third time was around the year 2009. I was juggling with all the demands of being on the leadership team of a church while having a growing family and working as a psychiatrist. It became too much for me to handle and something had to give. At the core was the fact that I did not like the person I had become. Sensing a critical and discontented spirit growing inside me, I knew it was time to step down from something and re-evaluate my priorities. At this point, I stepped aside from the church leadership.

In all three cases of burnout there were both significant learning opportunities and resulting growth from the experience. At the time, it felt very different to that!

After the first time, I experienced a spiritual awakening that continues to have an impact on me to this very day. After the second, I found a greater purpose and direction to stay in medicine and I began to focus on psychiatry. As for the third, it laid the foundation for starting a blog, podcasts, coaching and even this book!

Burnout is a state of chronic stress. It gradually develops over a period of time and leads to three main outcomes:

1. *Both physical and emotional exhaustion*

   On each occasion, I gradually found myself lacking energy, sleeping poorly and unable to give proper attention to what needed to be done.

2. *Feelings of cynicism and detachment*

   I was quick to focus on the negative aspects of my life and I felt disconnected from others. It caused me to attribute unnecessary ulterior motives to others and put myself in a victim mindset.

3. *Feelings of ineffectiveness and lack of accomplishment*

   I struggled to find meaning and purpose in day-to-day activities that became increasingly burdensome. What previously I had been able to do with ease felt like an upward struggle with no apparent end in sight.

DEPRESSION

Depression has been called the 'common cold' of psychological problems because nearly everyone has experienced it in some form at some time. The word 'depression' itself is, like stress, a confusing term. It is used frequently in day-to-day conversation and it's also used in what is intended to be a more precise, clinical way by doctors and psychiatrists.

According to the psychologist Martin Seligman, people born since 1945 are ten times more likely to suffer from depression than those born before. He estimated 350 million people around the world suffer from depression, which is the leading cause of disability and a major contributor to the burden of disease.[76]

Depression has been described as the number one psychological disorder in the Western world. It is said to be growing in all age groups in virtually every community. The growth is seen most in the young, especially amongst teens. This rate of increase led it to become, by 2020, the second-most disabling condition in the world, second only to heart disease.[77]

But because the word 'depression' is used so freely and interchangeably in many different ways, we need to be careful about explaining what the D-word actually means.

It's very common to experience feelings of sadness or distress in some way. These feelings may be a result of grief or other stresses in life, including physical illness. Sometimes feelings of sadness appear out of the blue with no obvious relationship to anything else going on in the person's life. There appears to be a spectrum of mood disturbance that can range from mild to severe and from short-lived episodes to long periods of unremitting illness.

Depression was recorded by the ancient Greeks, the Bible and Shakespeare, but it was only relatively recently, in 1980, that a formal definition came into being.[78] This was when the American Psychiatric Association produced what is called the *Diagnostic and Statistical Manual for Mental Disorders 3rd edition (DSM-III).*

The 5th edition (DSM-V) published in May 2013[79] lists the following criteria for the diagnosis of what is called a major depressive episode:

At least five of the following nine symptoms need to be present over a two-week period or longer:

- Depressed or irritable mood most of the day, nearly every day (feeling sad, empty, or tearful)
- A diminished interest or pleasure in all, or almost all, activities for most of the day nearly every day (psychiatrists call this anhedonia)
- Significant and unintended weight loss or weight gain (usually accompanied by a change in appetite)
- Extreme fatigue or loss of energy
- Significant changes in patterns of sleep (either too little or too much sleep)

- A slowing down of behaviour and speech that is noticeable by others (called psychomotor retardation) or the opposite, extreme agitation and restlessness (called psychomotor agitation)
- Feelings of worthlessness or guilt that are excessive and unwarranted
- Difficulty concentrating and making decisions
- Recurrent thoughts of death or suicide and/or making a plan to commit suicide

There are three further requirements to using the DSM-V for an official diagnosis of major depressive episodes:

- One of the five symptoms has to be either depressed mood or loss of pleasure.
- The symptoms have to represent a change from the person's normal level of functioning.
- The symptoms have to cause sufficient problems or distress in the person's life. This could be in the areas of making or keeping relationships or fulfilling work obligations.

From this point, the depression is classified as mild, moderate or major according to severity. But however the doctor classifies the depression, for the individual it is always major. Like all minor surgery, if it's happening to you personally, it is major surgery!

The other classification system is the ICD (International Classification of Diseases).[80] The ICD is produced by the World Health Organisation and is very similar to the DSM.

That is how psychiatrists and doctors diagnose depression. But it is still a challenge to making sense of what we mean exactly by the D-word.

Both the DSM and ICD set strict criteria for identifying disorders of the mind such as depression. You would think that such an approach would make diagnosis more reliable. In fact, there is much criticism about both these systems.

For example, why were five of the above symptoms chosen and not, say, four or six? Why two weeks and not three weeks? The decision to go for five symptoms over two weeks was judged appropriate, though arbitrary. The effect is that anyone who is consistently unhappy for a fortnight and also has other symptoms, such as poor sleep and loss of concentration, could be diagnosed as having a major depressive episode. It also means that the prevalence of the condition is very high, at up to 50% of people at some point over their lifetime!

This uncertainty explains why there are understandable concerns about wrongly diagnosing, or overdiagnosing, and thus ending up with medicalising so-called normal behaviour.

DSM-V has softened a number of exclusion criteria, particularly those for grief. The implication is that any symptoms that last for two weeks or longer must be an abnormal response. Genuine concerns have been expressed over what is a normal human experience of grief being medicalised into an illness.

So why is the diagnosis of depression increasing so much? It is the result of the combining together of the two different categories of sadness and depressive disorder.

According to a British Medical Journal review by Dowrick and Frances, overdiagnosis is more common than underdiagnosis.[81] They quote a study where only '38% of adults with clinician identified depression' actually met criteria for depression. That means that in more than half the cases, doctors are incorrectly diagnosing depression and are unnecessarily prescribing medication with the associated potential side effects and costs.

On a personal level, we don't know how to talk about our sadness or disappointments. We lurch into tasks and seek ways to medicate our pain. We escape into shopping, working, watching television, food binges, drugs or alcohol, fantasies or pornography, email and Facebook. In many churches, the unspoken rule is: 'You aren't spiritual if you're feeling depressed or sad'. So people pretend that all is well. The not-so-subtle message is that if you are following God properly, you are supposed to not feel hurt, confused or discouraged. What you need is simply more faith and if you were more diligent in your spiritual practices, then these feelings would go away.

For more on depression, do see drsunil.com/depression.

REGRET

So many people seem to be absorbed and focussed on their goals and achieving success regardless of the cost to their health and relationships. It's very easy to be focussed on a particular path in life to the exclusion of considering long-term implications.

There is an analogy (first attributed to Coca-Cola CEO Brian Dyson) of how life can be regarded as bouncing a series of five balls.[82] Each ball has a different label—health, family, friendship, work and one described as activities that nurture our soul. They are all made of fragile glass except the one called work, which is made of rubber. In other words, if you drop the health, family or friendships ball, (all activities that nurture the soul) they can each be irrevocably damaged. It is only the one called work that can bounce back if you drop it. The point of this analogy is not to excuse laziness at work, but to think about how we manage these five key 'balls'.

The consequences of not managing the non-work parts of life are vividly described in the immensely popular book by Australian nurse Bronnie Ware called *The Top Five Regrets of the Dying—A Life Transformed by the Dearly Departing.*[83] These top five regrets, as witnessed by Bronnie Ware, are:

> *1. I wish I'd had the courage to live a life true to myself, not the life others expected of me.*

Ware describes this absence of courage as the most common regret of all. With the realisation that life is almost over, there is an acute awareness of looking back and seeing how many dreams have gone unfulfilled. She estimates that for the majority of people the choices they had either made or omitted to make mean that they achieve less than half of their aspirations. Too easily do we take for granted the freedom which health gives us until we no longer have it.

2. I wish I hadn't worked so hard.

It is sobering that every male patient she nursed talked of this regret. They invariably spoke in terms of missing their children growing up and of their spouse's companionship. While women did also speak of this regret, most were from a past generation that had not worked outside of the home. There is much truth in the famous saying, 'No one on their death bed says I wish I had spent more time in the office'.

3. I wish I'd had the courage to express my feelings.

Another sad finding was how many had stifled their feelings in preference for adopting an attitude of stoicism to keep peace with others. This led to realising that their lives had become mediocre and far short of the potential which they knew that they were capable of. For many, this also led to bitterness and resentment manifesting as physical illness.

4. I wish I had stayed in touch with my friends.

Friendships are often taken for granted. For many, this need to contact old friends came in the last few weeks of life when, tragically, it was not always possible to track them down in time. It is very common to become so caught up in our own lives that precious friendships are not prioritised. Ware poignantly concludes, 'Everyone misses their friends when they are dying'.

5. I wish that I had let myself be happier.

Considering our culture's obsession with happiness, Ware found this was surprisingly common. For many people, the truth that happiness does not have to depend on external circumstances and can be a choice had somehow passed them by. Instead, they allowed themselves to stay stuck in familiar patterns and habits which came to dominate their existence. Because they were afraid of change, they had pretended to others and even to themselves that they were content when deep down they longed for child-like fun and laughter. Realising this on their deathbed was a sad moment, and too late.

Reading such an account is not easy. Yet thinking this through with clarity and logic can be enormously beneficial and powerful in planning how we can live our own lives with lasting success, fulfilment and the absence of regret. V. W. Burroughs said, 'One of the saddest experiences is to awaken at old age and discover that one has been using only a small part of the self'.[84] The sudden death of my very good friend Bunty in March 2014 drove this home to me forcefully. Since then I have slowly begun to realise how important it is to live with an acute awareness of one's own mortality. This is not for morbid reasons, but in order to make the most of the gift of life which we have been given.

DEATH AND SUICIDE

One of the great modern tragedies of a world that is challenging and complex is the increasing number of people who feel that life is not worth living. It's a difficult subject that gets relatively little coverage. Yet the statistics give a staggering indication of how widespread an issue it is.

The World Health Organisation estimates that worldwide approximately 800,000 people die by suicide every year.[85] There can be no doubt of the tragic consequences of such a final act. Suicide is a permanent solution to what in hindsight coupled with hope would often have been deemed to be temporary problems. Someone committing suicide can see no other alternative to the situation they find themselves in. It's the final devastating outcome of a belief that the only way out of the pain is to terminate one's life. In Western-style secular society what the person committing suicide often believes is that death will lead to an end of existence.

Paradoxically, this belief is a statement of faith, albeit one which many find strange.

Although suicide rates tend to increase with age there has recently been an alarming increase in suicidal behaviour amongst young people aged fifteen to twenty-five. This is happening not only in Western-style secular societies but across cultures worldwide.[86] With the exception of rural China and parts of India, more men than women successfully commit suicide, although in most places more women than men deliberately self-harm in what can appear to be attempted suicide. Suicide is now the leading cause worldwide of death for men aged fifteen to forty-nine. Men are three times more likely than women to take their own lives.[87,88]

Key factors associated with suicide in men include:

- Depression (especially when untreated or undiagnosed)
- Alcohol or drug misuse
- Unemployment
- Family and relationship problems (including marital breakup and divorce)

The National Confidential Inquiry into suicide by children and young people stated, 'Suicide is the second leading cause of death among 15–29-year-olds worldwide, accounting for 8% of all deaths in the UK. Suicide is the leading cause of death in young people, accounting for 14% of deaths in 10–19-year-olds and 21% of deaths in 20–34-year-olds'.[89]

United Kingdom statistics show that, in 2018, there were 6,507 suicides in the UK—an average of around eighteen people ending their own lives every day.[90]

The author and highly popular TED talk speaker Simon Sinek describes himself as an unshakeable optimist. However, when writing about the generation known as the baby boomers (born approximately between 1946–1964), he comes to some sobering conclusions. Baby boomers are growing increasingly disappointed and disillusioned with life in the world they find themselves a part of. Since the turn of the last century, the rate of suicide among this group has grown so dramatically that it now claims more deaths than car accidents and ranks third behind cancer and heart disease. His conclusion is that this is only likely to get worse for the post baby-boomer generations. His reason is that rather than relying on biological bonds of friendship and loving relationships, those who are 20–30 years younger than the baby boomers have grown up relying on social media, prescription drugs and online support groups as their main form of coping with the life which they see as presenting increasingly complex challenges. This disconnection from human relationships, he predicts, is likely to become manifest in rising rates of depression, prescription drug abuse and suicidal behaviour.[91]

My motivation for writing this book has been driven in part by wishing to provide an attractive alternative to the growing undercurrent of despair in many lives.

Any discussion of suicide also needs to cover a subject that is rarely debated openly. Coming from a South Asian background, I am very aware that there is an even darker side to suicide. That is the whole issue of suicide bombing and killings in the name of religion. Currently, this fervour seems to particularly affect the religion of Islam.

My own journey of faith from a Hindu background included a deep sense of emptiness and absence of meaning. I could not satisfy these feelings in the secular West European environment in which I was brought up. My adolescence and early adulthood coincided with the age which sought freedom but also lacked responsibility in both general behaviour and, particularly, sexual relationships. Part of me wanted that, while another more perceptive part could see that it led to an empty and dead-end future. My problem was that for a number of months in my late teens, I could see no alternative.

I am convinced that if I had been attracted to the clear rules and strong community support of Islam rather than coming to a living faith in Christ, I would have developed further my pride and sense of superiority towards Western culture. Unchecked, I could have gone on to use Islam to vent my fury with the world in a form of suicide terrorism. The sad reality is that this is how many in the Muslim world look at the West. The gap between cultures is widened by the secular Western mind struggling to define a category which will enable them to best address these emotions and longings. Western culture cannot fathom how, in pursuit of greater meaning and purpose, people resort to such evil acts in the belief that they will find reward in the life to come.

Someone who thought deeply about the implications of Western secular thinking was Czeslaw Milosz, the Nobel Prize winning Polish poet and author. Over a ninety year lifetime he experienced the repression of both Nazism and Communism. In the essay he wrote before his death, 'The Discreet Charms of Nihilism', he made a fascinating observation. Quoting Marx's well-known saying that 'religion is the opium of the masses,' he concluded that 'the true opium of the people is a belief in nothingness after death'. This nihilism led and possibly sanctioned many to ignore the consequences of their actions. Czeslaw Milosz followed with the acute observation, 'It's the huge solace of thinking that our betrayals, our greed, our cowardice, our murders, are not going to be judged. But all religions have recognised our deeds are imperishable'.[92]

Believing that there is nothing after death is a very secular idea. I am quite sure that this attitude to death feeds the desire, when life becomes unbearable, to completely stop existing by ending one's own life. The disconnection from responsibility to oneself and others progresses to the thought of escaping painful consequences which appear to lack any hope of resolution. Suicide becomes a permanent solution to problems which from another perspective are likely to seem temporary.

The underlying belief about suicide is that following death, existence will cease and everything will be over—this life is all that there is to live for. But such thinking does not satisfy the deep hunger and restlessness of our human souls, as it renders human existence meaningless. In reality, as long as there is life there is hope. Secular thinking resolutely refuses to pursue such lines of thinking. That is why we need wisdom to lead us away from the hollow promises that are based on secular and materialistic ideas.

THE PROBLEM OF EVIL

One of the great dilemmas of modern societies which lacks a spiritual grounding is how to make sense of the evil and the suffering we either experience ourselves or see others endure. The author W. H. Auden faced this dilemma just as World War II was breaking out. Before the War, he had left Europe for the United States. He considered himself to be an atheist. In November 1939, at a cinema in a largely German-speaking area of New York, he watched a documentary by the Nazis of their conquest of Poland. He was disturbed to see the reaction of many of those in the cinema around him. When the screen began to show Poles he was shocked to hear many in the audience scream, 'Kill them!' Up to that point, he had believed in the popular mindset of the un-religious of the age that people are basically good and that the only requirement for them to lead a decent life is the right education and upbringing. Yet in that cinema, in an instant, he was brought to the realisation that such thinking was inadequate. His secular thinking, which had no belief in moral goodness, lacked any wisdom with which to legitimately object to the inhumanity he felt around him (or, indeed, the crimes of the Nazis themselves) if people were just expressing their innate evil. As he put it, 'There had to be some reason why [Hitler] was utterly wrong'.[93]

But his Western liberal, secular upbringing could offer no answer. For Auden, the liberal thinking of pre-war England was inadequate to this task. Later, in 1940, he wrote:

> *The whole trend of liberal thought . . . has been to undermine faith in the absolute . . . It has tried to make reason the judge . . . but since life is a changing process . . . the attempt to find a humanistic basis for keeping a promise, works logically with*

> *the conclusion, 'I can break it whenever I feel it convenient'.*[94]

More than eighty years after Auden delivered his insights, we still live with a dogged and determinedly atheistic view of the world that is continually coming up short in accounting for and understanding the complexity and tragedies of life.

BRINGING IT ALL TOGETHER

Perhaps the saddest consequence of the confusion and complexity around us is when we allow the life and dreams within ourselves to die silently inside us.

There is a painful internal resignation that runs through a life which has no zest nor sense of anticipation nor excitement. Everything that happens in such a life is closely fenced in by the lacklustre motion of routine and predictability. We are afraid of stepping away from the conventional or socially acceptable and we are afraid of being found out getting it wrong. Part of this timidness is because we do not know how to cope with failure. We struggle with the prospect of getting things wrong and failing because we are too emotionally invested in a particular outcome. Our identity and self-worth are at risk if we fail to get what we want. As I've grown older, I have been struck by how much this is the experience of the older generation. We sense something of all of this anxiety and caution in life. The result is a life that we find frustrating, at times pointless, and profoundly exhausting.

Over a hundred years ago Oswald Chambers commented on someone he had met ten years previously and admired for their earnest devotion and commitment to the ways of God. Meeting the same person a second time a decade later, Chambers was shocked to find this person, as he puts it, 'Garrulous and unenlivened'.[95] In other words, they would talk excessively about trivial matters in a way that was dull and uninteresting. He concluded:

> *How many men seem to become like that after forty years of age! The fear of sloth and indulgence has come home with a huge fear and fairly driven me to God to keep me from ever forgetting what I owe Him.*[96]

Some of the words Chambers' uses seem from a bygone era. But I find them challenging and worth pondering over. He is commenting on someone he met who, over a period of ten years, changed from being passionate and zealous for the things of God to being excessively talkative about things that are trivial and unimportant. This person had become dull and uninteresting, excessively preoccupied with themselves. His life had become small-minded and inconsequential. As someone comfortably over the age of forty, it is jolting to read Chambers' assessment that this is a common phenomenon over the age of forty!

In my experience, the problem that Chambers identified has not diminished but has grown more prevalent with time.

Our culture and age emphasise ease, rest and comfort above all else. Another word for that is 'sloth'. Dorothy Sayers defines *sloth* as 'the sin which believes in nothing, cares for nothing, seeks to know nothing, interferes with nothing, enjoys nothing, loves nothing, hates nothing, finds purpose in nothing, lives for nothing, and only remains alive because there is nothing it would die for'.[97] I confess to seeing such a tendency within myself. I do not think I am alone in that. But, what a tragic way to live life!

The majority of people regard their day-to-day work as a toil and drudgery that has to be tolerated until either the weekend releases them or occasional holidays materialise. Work is a necessary burden to bear until escaping to really live and enjoy life. Sadly, this unending routine seems to be the rhythm of life for very many people. But our restless hearts, our questioning minds and our disordered lives need more; they need wisdom.

The bigger issue is the question of ego. The ego is an internal enemy which each one of us has to deal with. Ego prevents us truly living in wisdom and traps us within ourselves.

In the next chapter, we will look at the question of ego.

REVIEW QUESTIONS TO CONSIDER

1. Discontentment, fear, dread, shame, worry, anxiety, loneliness are all common human feelings and emotions. How do I handle them in my own life and those of others?
2. Stress and burnout are common experiences of many people in our fast-paced world. How can I protect myself from its negative effects?
3. How much have I experienced feelings of depressive thinking or this 'common cold' of psychological problems? What has helped me?
4. What can I begin to do today to ensure that I do not live life with regret?
5. Our restless hearts, questioning minds and disordered lives can lead to any one or combination of the painful manifestations discussed in this chapter. Which one raises the most questions for me?

PART 2

Developing Wisdom

"Wisdom is knowledge with the Knower left in."

—Anonymous

4
MANAGING OUR EGO

Why do we find it so difficult to accept the truth? Because we are looking for bargains. We want shortcuts. There are no easy ways. There is only one way. If we are going to be complete human beings, we are going to have to do it with God. We will have to be rescued from these despotic egos . . . We will have to expose the life of self-centredness and proclaim the truth of God-centredness.

—Eugene Peterson, *Run with Horses*

THE PROBLEM OF EGO

When we talk of someone having an ego, we're more than just stating a fact and we're certainly not offering them a compliment!

The truth is that we all have an ego. But what do we mean by the word ego and, on our quest for wisdom, why can it cause such great problems in our own lives and the lives of others? Is there such a thing as a healthy amount of ego? If so, we will need much wisdom to get that balance right!

All of us struggle with the problem of ego. When I use the word ego, I am not necessarily saying that it is all bad and unhealthy. In the right portion, our ego is inherently positive and provides a healthy level of confidence and ambition. When ego works well, it drives out insecurity, fear, sloth and apathy. But left unchecked, it can spiral out of control and grow easily into arrogance. When that happens, it becomes destructive by attacking our talents and abilities. This destruction is either through overconfidence and giving the false illusion that we're better than we actually are, or by robbing us of confidence to the extent that we lose trust in our ability to use those talents to capacity.

At one extreme, the tendency of ego to make us think too little of ourselves pushes us into the trap of not valuing who we are and the contribution we can make. At the other extreme, we find the obvious problem of thinking more highly of ourselves than is appropriate. That can lead to making foolish decisions and trampling insensitively over the feelings, plans or ideas of others. There are more occasions than I feel comfortable to admit when I have allowed pride to influence decisions which I later regretted. More close to home, when my wife has tried lovingly to challenge me I have often been too proud to listen.

Football manager Jose Mourinho is known for being disarmingly honest. He illustrates the danger of pride with his comments on a Spanish radio station in 2011 when asked what he felt God thought of him:

> *He must really think I'm a great guy. He must think that, because otherwise He would not have given me so much. I have a great family. I work in a place where I've always dreamt of working. He has helped me out so much that He must have a very high opinion of me.*[98]

Before we pass judgement on Mourinho, let's reflect for a moment. For all of us it is very easy to fall into Mourinho's way of thinking when things go well in life. We attribute what we have to our own inherent goodness or ability, putting ourself at the centre and therefore somehow worthy of God's attention and love. At the same time, it is worth pondering, as Mourinho admits, that God must have a high opinion of us if he allows us to continue existing in a world where there is also such a high level of sorrow and negativity.

WISDOM IN FINDNG THE RIGHT BALANCE OF EGO

Somewhere around the mid-point between thinking too highly and too little of oneself there is humility that keeps our ego balanced between these two extremes.

John Newton (1725–1807) was a slave trader who lived a life of gambling, drinking and a reckless disregard for other people. He experienced a spiritual awakening which led to a radical change in the direction of his life and eventually to him writing the famous hymn 'Amazing Grace'. A favourite saying of his captures living with humility while keeping one's ego in check: *By the grace of God, I am what I am. I am not what I want to be, but I thank God I am not what I once was.*[99]

What is liberating about this perspective is the tension between accepting who he is with all his failures and struggles while at the same time acknowledging there is a long way to go. The key that holds this tension together for us is being grateful for how far we have already come. William Law, back in the 18th century, said 'Every good thought that we have, and every good action that we perform, lays us open to pride and thus exposes us to the various assaults of vanity and self-satisfaction'.[100] Those words hold as true today as they were then. In these ten contrasting statements, what tendencies do you see in yourself?

You parade in public what should be kept private.
You are far too self-referencing.
You talk when you should shut up.
You are quiet when you should speak.

You care too much about what people think about you.
You care too little about what people think about you.
You resist facing and admitting your sins/weaknesses/failures.
You struggle with appreciating and celebrating the success of others.
You are more position orientated than submission orientated.
You believe you are in control of your life.

All of us are guilty of falling into any of these extremes at one time or another. We can be so preoccupied with ourselves that even the good that we do leads to a sense of superiority or aloofness to others. However subtle they are, the seeds and roots are in all of us. If allowed to germinate and grow in our hearts, they can cause great damage to the lives of us and those around us. It's helpful to tease out the connection between ego and pride.

UNPACKING EGO AND PRIDE

The word 'ego' comes from Latin, where it means 'I, myself'.[101] Psychologists talk of the ego as the conscious part of the mind that sits between the id (the primitive part of the mind preoccupied with immediate gratification) and the super-ego (our internal moral policeman telling us what is right and wrong). So ego is an inflated sense of self-importance but it's also closely linked to self-confidence. That implies ego can also have a positive meaning. While there is a risk of being a deep liability it can also be a valuable asset. Jim Collins, one of the most prolific business authors of the last sixty years, talks about this in his book *Good to Great* with the concept of Level 5 Leadership.

In his research, Collins found that two-thirds of the companies that don't make the leap from 'Good' to 'Great' were weighed down by what he described as 'the presence of gargantuan personal ego that contributed to the demise or continued mediocrity of the company'. For the eleven companies that made the leap from good to great, Collins described two unique traits of their leaders:

- Intense professional will
- Extreme personal humility[102]

There is something intensely powerful about combining these two apparently contrasting qualities of fierce determination and a distinct lack of self-absorption. "Humility in the true sense is not thinking less of oneself, but simply thinking of oneself less". That is a radical thought and worth reading again!

When we talk about someone having an ego, we mean that person is so self-absorbed that they cannot see anything else. It gets more complicated than that! The dictionary definition of ego talks about 'a person's sense of self-esteem or self-importance'.[103] Another way of describing that is pride. In terms of what pride is, the dictionary describes 'a feeling of deep pleasure or satisfaction derived from one's own achievements, the achievements of one's close associates, or from qualities or possessions that are widely admired'.[104] As with ego, there is both a negative and a positive side to pride.

If we start with the negative aspect, there are stark warnings. In one of his books, C. S. Lewis devotes a whole chapter to describing pride as 'The Great Sin'.

> *There is one vice of which no man in the world is free; which everyone in the world knows when he sees it in someone else; and of which hardly any people ... ever imagine that they are guilty of themselves.... The essential vice, the utmost evil is pride. Unchastity, anger, greed, drunkenness, and all that are mere flea bites in comparison; it was through pride that the devil became the devil; pride leads to every other vice; it is the complete anti-God state of mind.*[105]

This is the fragile over-inflated ego that is preoccupied with self and how we come across to others. It is a constant unwavering self-absorption that puts us at the centre of the universe. Everything that happens in the world is brought back to ourself and how it makes us feel or where we stand in relation to others. This kind of pride is always looking down on others and seeks to find ways to feel superior or better.

There is an alternative way of looking at things.

Isak Dinesen teases this out positively by describing healthy pride as 'faith in the idea God had when he made us'.[106] When we grasp that profound statement we incorporate the divine calling into all our strivings and aspirations. Our yearnings for success, significance and comfort have to include what God ultimately wants for us. What that leads to for the appropriately proud is, according to Dinesen:

> *His success is the idea of God, successfully carried through, and he is in love with his destiny. As the good citizen finds his happiness in the fulfilment of his duty to the community, so does the proud man find his happiness in the fulfilment of his fate.*[107]

A good way to think of a healthy level of pride and ego is that it is rather like thinking absent-mindedly about your fingers or toes! Tim Keller talks of this in terms of a 'gospel-humble person':

> *The truly gospel-humble person is a self-forgetful person whose ego is just like his or her toes. It just works. It does not draw attention to itself. The toes just work; the ego just works. Neither draws attention to itself.*[108]

> "HEALTHY PRIDE IS FAITH IN THE IDEA GOD HAD WHEN HE MADE US".

This is a delightful sense of self-forgetfulness, whereby you live, speak and behave as you are made to without feeling a need to prove or downplay yourself.

"Healthy pride is faith in the idea God had when He made us".

HOW DO I DEVELOP THE WISDOM TO RECOGNISE WHEN MY EGO IS GETTING OUT OF CONTROL?

I've often laughed at Theodore Roosevelt's famous saying "If you could kick the person in the pants responsible for most of your trouble, you wouldn't sit for a month".[109] It takes an enormous amount of self-awareness, even courage, to recognise and acknowledge responsibility for our failings and mistakes. It is much easier to blame others or look for fault elsewhere.

Let me introduce a globally influential thinker on leadership. Marshall Goldsmith is arguably one of the most insightful and successful business coaches in the world. In a short, punchy and profound four-minute video available at drsunil.com/ego, he touches on the important subject of ego and how it can get in the way of us living truly satisfying and fulfilling lives.[110]

His provocative point is that every day we make ego and pride (putting myself and my desires ahead of anyone or anything else) more important than our health, our safety and even the people we claim to love. Pride is the ultimate form of selfishness. That selfishness is the worst part of human nature. Tim Keller, referencing C. S. Lewis, vividly describes it as, 'A ruthless sleepless unsmiling concentration on the self'.[111] This is no small or trivial issue. It often manifests itself through a blind spot that affects all of us in some way or another. Pride has destroyed countless individuals, families and even nations.

In the Marshall Goldsmith video at drsunil.com/ego, he uses the example of surgeons in operating theatres. A study by Atul Gawande found that not allowing nurses to ask a series of simple questions of the surgeons such as 'Did you wash your hands?' and simply failing to systematise such questions into a basic checklist has contributed to more deaths than the Vietnam War, Afghan War and Iraq War combined! That is a staggering claim.

The positive way forward advocated in the video is to appeal to enlightened self-interest. A pilot, for example, being asked by a junior simple questions from a checklist such as 'How much fuel do you have?' is vital to prevent not just needless passenger deaths but also the death of the pilot himself. Similarly, but less dramatically, when we let our ego win not only us but everyone else loses.

The vast majority of us are not surgeons or pilots. How can we better arm ourselves in our daily lives against the dangerous self-sabotaging effects of our egos? The best way is to recognise and be aware of the early warning signs before they cause irreparable and lasting damage. Warning signs include these four:

1—Playing the comparison game

This is the tendency to compare ourselves to others and to find ways to put ourself above or below them in some way. We tend to pit our strengths against another's weaknesses, or reverse this by comparing our weaknesses to their strengths. When we do the former, we feel superior or morally better. When we do the latter, we become discouraged or disillusioned with life and ourselves. Both paths ultimately distance us from others and create an impenetrable wall of aloofness.

2—Being defensive

There is an important distinction between defending an idea and being defensive. When we are defending an idea, our motive is to let the best argument win. We should understand that nobody knows everything, especially in an increasingly complex and challenging world. The best decisions are the result of rigorous and independent thinking followed by passionate, collaborative debate. However, when we are being defensive, we are so identified with our idea that any challenge becomes a personal attack. We might refuse to back down as a way to protect our fragile ego. If our idea loses, we lose personally.

3—Needing to display our brilliance

Once again, there is an important distinction. Yes, we want to perform to the best of our ability and reach our maximum potential. The danger presents itself when we seek to be the centre of attention and devote excessive time and energy to that. Albert Einstein, with an unquestionably brilliant mind, said '... certainly we should take care not to make the intellect our god; it has, of course, powerful muscles, but no personality. It cannot lead, it can only serve.' [112] We can easily focus on our intellect to the expense of everything else. Simply knowing more than other people can lead to a sense of superiority over them.

4—Needing to be liked and accepted

It is not inherently wrong to want to be respected, liked and accepted. Those are positive fundamental needs that make our lives better. However, when we become oversensitive to what people think of us, we are prevented from being true to ourselves. That, in turn, subordinates speaking our mind behind personal promotion or public opinion. If we don't say what we really think because we fear losing respect, likeability or acceptance, we de-value our own ideals and principles. This is very subtle; we need to be particularly sensitive to it.

Egotistical pride has been described as the worst of all sins because it's the one sin that completely devastates relationships. As C. S. Lewis points out, a group of thieves or murderers while committing terrible crimes can still be friends and show loving self-sacrifice for each other. However, a group of proud people can ultimately never do so, for the moment one of them steps out of line, they have to be ejected from the group.[113]

This is why recognising the seeds of pride in ourself becomes so important. Susanna Wesley's words (1669-1742) are powerful and resonant:

> *Whatever weakens your reason, impairs the tenderness of your conscience, obscures your sense of God, takes off your relish for spiritual things, whatever increases the authority of the body over the mind, that thing is sin to you, however innocent it may seem in itself.*[114]

Living in this tension between having gratitude for how far we have come while recognising how far we still have to go is a hallmark of real humility.

LEARNING TO GROW IN HUMILITY

But what exactly is humility? The English word humility comes from the Latin *humilitas* and means 'from the earth'.[115] It is about being appropriately grounded in oneself, thinking neither too highly nor too little of oneself.

One of the problems with the word is that it tends to be associated more with the negative than the positive. We are inclined to think of humility in terms of not being arrogant or boastful or not putting yourself above others. The best definition I have come across originated with Ralph Washington Sockman, who was a senior pastor of Christ Church in New York City:

> *True humility is intelligent self-respect which keeps us from thinking too highly or too meanly of ourselves. It makes us modest by reminding us how far we have come short of what we can be.*[116]

To put it even more succinctly humility is not thinking less of oneself, but rather thinking of oneself less. Its polar opposite is pride, vividly and disturbingly defined by C. S. Lewis as 'a ruthless sleepless unsmiling concentration on the self'.[117] That short, punchy phrase captures the terror of a pride that takes itself far too seriously and sees the whole universe as revolving around itself. A self-centredness that has to be protected at all costs, with no room for displaying weakness or vulnerability.

There is a temptation to think that the opposite of displaying too much ego is to be humble. The problem with too little ego is that we fail to value ourselves and the important contribution we can make on so many levels to those around us. There is a general lack of confidence in ourself and a loss of appropriate self-esteem. Striking the right level of ego involves a healthy tension between the following three areas:

- Considering 'we' first, and then following with 'me' (devotion to progress)
- Holding the thought 'I'm brilliant,' and 'I'm not' simultaneously (the principle of duality)
- There will always be one more thing to improve (constructive discontent)

According to the behavioural theory authors Marcum and Smith, the deepest level of humility is at the intersection of these three domains.[118] The challenge is keeping all three in equilibrium. When we are around this centre our talents stay true to form and we are able to make our greatest contribution. However, we all have a natural tendency to wander from the equilibrium. As we move away from the centre we begin to lose the power of humility, and our apparent strengths then become weaknesses that masquerade as strengths.

If you have followed me thus far, you may be saying that this sounds all rather abstract to everyday life. C. S. Lewis's description of what it looks like to meet a truly humble person makes these ideas more practical. He boils it down to two simple characteristics. Firstly, that they appear remarkably content and happy with themselves. They are not trying to prove anything to you, to anyone else or to themselves. They are content with being who they are. Secondly, you will notice that they are very interested in you, your concerns and your priorities in such a way that they seem to practically forget about themselves.[119]

EGO AND THE FOOL

Another way to talk about this is to refer to the fool. In our day and culture, the word fool is used as a dismissive insult. Ideas of what is a fool vary. In Western culture, a fool is often symbolised as a donkey while in India the symbol of a fool is an owl—an animal that is regarded as wise in the West! [120] Foolishness, regardless of culture, is the opposite of wisdom.

When we call someone a fool we want to have nothing to do with them and their so-called foolish behaviour. The reality is we all act as fools at one time or another. I dare say that there are aspects of foolish thinking and behaviour in our lives right now that we are not even aware of!

There is much to be gained from unpacking what we actually mean by the word *fool*. The word doesn't refer to someone with a lack of intelligence, a common misconception. It's very possible to have a high IQ and still behave like a fool. More straightforwardly a fool is someone who is habitually out of touch with reality. They make life miserable for themselves and those around them. Putting their ego at the centre of their life they have a destructive self-centredness.

Humility, by contrast, takes the ego away from the centre and is able to put God with His plans and purposes at the centre.

This prayer beautifully illustrates true humility and living in wisdom:

> *I am no longer my own, but yours.*
> *Put me to what you will, rank me with whom you will;*
> *Put me to doing; put me to suffering:*
> *Let me be employed for you, or laid aside for you,*
> *exalted for you or brought low for you;*
> *Let me be full, let me be empty*
> *Let me have all things, let me have nothing:*

I freely and wholeheartedly yield all things to your pleasure and disposal.
And now glorious and blessed God, Father, Son and Holy Spirit,
You are mine and I am yours.[121]

REVIEW QUESTIONS TO CONSIDER

1. How aware are you of the effect of your own ego in your life?
2. How can you develop the wisdom to sense your ego is getting out of control?
3. When do you find yourself becoming defensive, playing the comparison game or needing to show others how apparently brilliant you are? List some occasions.
4. How comfortable are you with 'faith in the idea God had when He made me'?[122]

5

REMOVING OUR IDOLS

The human heart is an idol factory.

—Martin Luther (1483-1546)

Why do we tend to veer off into foolishness? None of us deliberately tells ourselves that we want to be foolish but we can so easily slip away from our chosen path. Like two lines that initially appear parallel but in reality are not, it's only a matter of time before those paths will be far apart. The longer and further those lines travel, the more widely separated they become and they end up headed in completely different directions. The same can be said of our walk with God and what He intends for us as we journey with Him. It's easy to veer away from the path He intends for us. No one reaches a destination they have always intended to get to if they allow themselves to drift. Without intense discipline or a system of continuous feedback, it's very easy to veer off course.

Idolatry is an important root of foolishness and a major reason for us to go off course. When we think of idols, our minds can wander in two basic directions. The first is to the latest celebrity singer from, say, a famous worldwide TV show popularised by Simon Cowell. Secondly, it is natural to think of statues of maybe stone, wood or marble that people bow down to. These are both forms of idolatry. What is common is the sense of awe and reverence given to either gifted human beings or to lifeless statues.

The Old Testament is full of warnings about the dangers of idolatry, along with the logic of why it's so foolish. In a carefully thought-through deconstruction of idols in the 7th century BC, the Old Testament prophet Isaiah carefully describes the work of a blacksmith and a carpenter. Through this explanation, he shows us both their human skill and their frailty. The point he seeks to drive home is that part of the wood the carpenter uses is for firewood and the rest is used to make an idol to which is attributed supernatural power. His analysis is penetrating:

> *Half of the wood he burns in the fire; over it he prepares his meal; he roasts his meat and eats his fill. He also warms himself and says, 'Ah! I am warm; I see the fire'.*
>
> *From the rest he makes a god, his idol; he bows down to it and worships. He prays to it and says, 'Save me! You are my god!'*

(The conclusion is also just as devastating.)

> *They know nothing, they understand nothing;*
> *their eyes are plastered over so that they cannot see,*
> *and their minds closed so that they cannot understand . . .*
> *Such a person feeds on ashes; a deluded heart misleads him;*
> *he cannot save himself, or say,*
> *'Is not this thing in my right hand a lie?*
>
> Isaiah ch 44 v16–18, 20

When described in such a way, it's easy to see the foolishness of idols. How can something so clearly manmade have any real power? Isaiah graphically describes how the craftsman uses half of the material to make a fire and warm himself while the other half he worships and attributes supernatural power. Isaiah wants to show us how absurd this is. Yet even though this was written almost three millenia ago, the problem of idolatry remains today.

Coming from a South Asian background, I've seen many temples with idols and statues to which the faithful bow down and worship. When I discuss this with Hindu friends and family, I am told that they're not worshipping the statue but what is behind the statue. The statue, I am told, is a metaphor for a greater and deeper power. To me, that still sounds like idolatry. But there is also much more to this. It affects all of us no matter what our background, professed religious faith or even absence of faith.

To unpack this, let's reflect on what we think an idol is. A broader definition is that it is anything more important to you than God, anything that absorbs your heart and imagination more than God does or anything you seek to give to you what only God can give. That includes looking to your own wisdom and competence or to some other creation to provide the power, approval, comfort and security that ultimately only God can provide.

An idol is whatever you look at and causes you to say in your heart of hearts, 'If I have that, then I'll feel my life has meaning; then I'll know I have value; then I'll feel significant and secure'. It's important to understand that this does not necessarily mean that it is bad. But described this way, examples such as money, sex and power can become obvious idols when we allow them to take over our hearts and imaginations. They become a source of longing and hope for our hearts and lead us to being enticed in their power and grip. Unchecked, they can bring great harm and devastation to our lives. But the same can be said also about apparently good things such as family, career and health. If any of these become too important in our lives, if we put too much expectation and meaning onto them, we will find ourselves eventually disappointed and frustrated. While we may appear to succeed in enjoying these things for long periods of time, sooner or later we will find ourselves disappointed or frustrated by them. If that doesn't happen during this life, it has to happen at the point of exiting this life. As these earthly things in which we put our expectation and confidence are finite they cannot last to infinity.

There is no limit to what our hearts can make into idols. Many centuries ago, Martin Luther described the human heart as an idol factory.[123] Our hearts continually put weight and significance on objects and desires that cannot ultimately deliver all that our hearts long and hope for. Our hearts can't live in a vacuum—they have to give significance and worth in order to mean something to us. The New Testament word which encapsulates this is *epithumia.*[124] Literally, this means over-desire, an all-controlling drive and longing. This is revealing. The main problem of our heart is not only desire for bad things but our over-desire for good things. We turn created, good things into gods and objects which we worship and serve.

There are many ways to describe that kind of relationship to something, but perhaps the best one is to call it 'worship'. When we use the word worship, we mean giving ultimate worth and value to something or someone. In the original Hebrew, the picture is of bowing down and kissing the feet of a king. We tend to think of worship as singing in a church or religious context, but it is also much deeper than that.

When we worship someone or something, we give it our committed attention and focus. It's where our minds go to when we have nothing in particular to think about. Worship is primarily an activity of the heart seeking rest and consolation. One of the best explanations of worship I have come across comes, surprisingly, not from a religious teacher but from an atheist American author and professor of English, David Foster Wallace. He gave a commencement speech to the graduating class at the Ohio liberal arts campus Kenyon College in 2005.[125] Speaking in a secular context, he made the startling claim that in the reality of day-to-day life, there is no such thing as atheism and not worshipping something. The only choice we have, he told the graduating students, is what we choose to worship.

Whatever we choose to worship has a huge influence on how we live and what we pursue with our ambition. The danger in such worship is that we can become completely consumed by what has captured our imagination. If, for example, I worship money, I will always feel that I never have enough no matter how much I make. Similarly many of the people whom we think of as the most beautiful in the world privately talk of how ugly and insecure they feel. At the back of our minds, we know an idol cannot ultimately satisfy our longings, but that realisation is so often hidden from our awareness. The problems we have in our relationships with others, such as wanting control or power over them, reflects the fear that what we actually worship, our own ego and self-elevation, is at risk of being lost. The result? We can refuse to talk even to our spouse about a particular subject, or we have to protect our fragile ego by finding others to ridicule or blame or put down.

Foster Wallace describes these attitudes as unconscious default settings. We lapse into them without thinking. 'They're the kind of worship you just gradually slip into, day after day, getting more and more selective about what you see and how you measure value without ever being fully aware what you're doing'. [126]

What's so powerful about this explanation is that it unpacks how, at our core, we are creatures with a need to worship. We are continually attaching ultimate value, or over-desire, to something or someone who will meet all of our needs and aspirations. The problem is that nothing can ultimately satisfy. You may recall the previous comments we made about disappointment. Such disappointment points to deeper unfulfilled desires. The danger is that the sorrow that we can feel when we are disappointed can turn into despair if what we have put our hopes onto becomes an idol. With sorrow, there is the possibility of consolation. What makes despair so deadly is that there's no prospect of consolation. At its extreme, despair can lead to suicide. The tragic conclusion of David Foster Wallace's life was that despite all this amazingly perceptive analysis he went on to commit suicide.

As we discussed in chapter 3, social commentators talk about how we appear to be entering an almost epidemic of suicide in the wealthier parts of the world. People who commit or attempt to commit suicide are displaying a loss of hope in what they previously put their trust and confidence in. Whatever it was that they believed in, it can no longer fulfil the desires and longings of the human heart.

But these longings we have also point to deeper mysteries of life. I touched on something of that in the Preface, describing my own life when I turned thirty-six.

These longings and desires point to something beyond ourselves. C. S. Lewis vividly describes how, in the physical world, we can see instances where the longing of our desires is fulfilled. A baby cries in hunger for food and is satisfied by being given milk. Baby ducklings instinctively want to swim, which is why they go to water. Erotic arousal and desires seek fulfilment in all sorts of sexual experience.

But what about those desires which never seem quite enough to satisfy? If all our hope for satisfaction is in an earthly desire, it never seems quite enough. We live in the most technologically advanced stage of human history. Increasing numbers of people all around the world have access to a variety of resources and opportunities through technology that would have amazed and staggered previous generations. We can eat an almost limitless variety of food; we can travel around the world to distant and exotic places at relatively low cost; we can communicate instantaneously with friends and family around the world. Yet, the nagging question is . . . are we any happier than previous generations who had so much less than we do? More of the same is not guaranteed to produce more happiness and contentment. Have we fallen for the misguided idea that the more we consume the happier we will be?

C. S. Lewis's conclusion is that if you have desires and longings, no experience in this world can satisfy them. They are not in us by accident. No other creature has this kind of restlessness. We do not see dogs longing for more than their most basic needs. The most logical explanation is one which our secular world is determined to ignore—that we were made for another world. Lewis's hypothesis is that unsatisfied human desires have been planted in us as signposts to something beyond this world. While it is right and proper to be thankful for and enjoy the world we are in, we do so remembering they are 'only a kind of copy, or echo, or mirage'.[127] He concludes:

> *I must keep alive in myself the desire for my true country, which I shall not find till after death; I must never let it get snowed under or turned aside; I must make it the main object of life to press on to that country and to help others to do the same.*[128]

Idols are a poor substitute for what, ultimately, only God can provide. We think that the lure of idols is too strong. In reality we have lost perspective on how the living God is so much more wonderful and satisfying than anything which we could wish or hunger for. Here is how C. S. Lewis puts it:

> *It would seem that Our Lord finds our desires not too strong, but too weak. We are half-hearted creatures, fooling about with drink and sex and ambition when infinite joy is offered us, like an ignorant child who wants to go on making mud pies in a slum because he cannot imagine what is meant by the offer of a holiday at the sea. We are far too easily pleased.*[129]

WISDOM IS BEING ON A PATH LEADING US TO LASTING SUCCESS, SATISFACTION AND SIGNIFICANCE.

The essence of foolishness is putting confidence in those manmade things that ultimately fail to deliver. Wisdom is being on a path leading us to lasting success, satisfaction and significance. It means shifting what we worship from the temporary and transient things of this world to the One who is eternal and can truly satisfy. We can summarise idolatry in the Bible as looking to our own wisdom and competence, or to some other created thing, to provide the power, approval, comfort and security we long for but which only God can provide.

The implication is that if my heart is an idol factory, if idolatry is such a natural tendency of my heart, it becomes necessary for me to recognise when I am veering into this idolatry. We can see that it is important to develop the wisdom skill of recognising when I am veering into idolatry. It is easy to say that we believe in God but still trust in something else for our real significance and happiness. Whatever that 'something else' is has become our real God. We have become experts at hiding this from ourselves. It is only when something goes wrong with, say, our career or family that we realise there are other things which have become more important to us than the God we claim to trust.

> AN IMPORTANT WISDOM SKILL IS THE ABILITY TO RECOGNISE WHEN I AM VEERING INTO IDOLATRY.

This is where the discipline of self-examination becomes so important. Those things we actually trust and have put our hopes in are surrounded by strong emotions. What are those things causing us to feel easily angry or despondent? They are those pointing to a goal or outcome we cannot reach and are feeling frustrated about. It may well be a noble and worthy ideal, but our emotional reaction can point towards attaching an excessive weight to what we think is the right outcome. Although it is easy to justify to ourself that our anger and indignation are appropriate and measured, are we, in reality, just putting ourself in a position of superiority and self-righteousness? This can be so deceptively subtle. The danger with excessive emotions is that they cloud our judgement and distort our vision of ourself and the world. This, in turn, leads to foolish decisions and a path away from wisdom. The path of wisdom, in this case, should follow our fears and frustrations to unmask those idols controlling us.

The Scottish churchman Thomas Chalmers (1780-1847) described the secret of the only way to displace idols from our hearts—'*by shifting our hearts to a greater love*'.[130]

THE PATH OF WISDOM INCLUDES FOLLOWING YOUR FEARS AND FRUSTRATIONS TO UNMASK THOSE IDOLS CONTROLLING YOU.

My conclusion is that no greater love is shown than in the Jewish carpenter who chose to lay down His life for mankind. As we grasp how much Christ has sacrificed for us, how He has descended, literally, to the depths of hell for us, we will begin finding the power to displace the idols of our heart for a greater love. You may have noticed that I have used the word *begin* to describe this process of dethroning our idols and replacing them with love for Christ. That is because this process is never-ending and will take our entire life.

REVIEW QUESTIONS TO CONSIDER

1. How aware are you of the idols you have created in your own heart and are looking to for meaning and satisfaction?
2. How much do you grasp that the longings of your own heart cannot ultimately be fulfilled in this life?
3. What do you think has become your God in place of the One you should really worship?
4. What is controlling how you currently live?

6
CHALLENGING OUR ASSUMPTIONS

I never let school interfere with my education.

—Mark Twain

As we try to get a handle on wisdom, it's important to get past some of the myths and fallacies that can permeate our thinking and culture. For this reason, unlearning much of what our culture and society has taught us becomes as important as learning about wisdom. Wisdom is not the same as information, knowledge or even knowing what to do. The popular television shows asking contestants about obscure and often trivial facts are not testing wisdom. Nor do games such as the famous Trivial Pursuit, which tests a person's knowledge of obscure information, have anything to do with wisdom. Instead, wisdom is the proper application of knowledge. Expressed another way, if science is organised knowledge, then wisdom is a truly organised life.

The first myth is that wisdom is only good, old-fashioned, plain common sense. I have to disagree. Common sense is certainly not just common practice; what appears to be obvious is often later either discredited or not followed through. Think, for example, about how easy it is for any of us to criticise our family about not doing a certain household chore while at the same time excusing ourselves as we're too tired or busy!

On a global level, every day we throw away more food in our homes, restaurants and supermarkets than it would take to feed the nearly one billion people who go hungry. We all know we should be able to love and respect one another, but that has not prevented centuries of ever increasing examples of global systemic racism, corruption, pollution, violence, war, inequality and injustice continuing to cause pain right across our world.

Then there is the knowledge-doing gap. It has been described as the greatest gap in the world. 'To know and not do is not to know.' How often, if we are honest with ourselves, have we known what we should do but found ourselves unable or even unwilling to do it? True wisdom is knowing what should be done in a context or situation and actually following through and doing it. Not talking about it or thinking about it or even feeling positive about it, but actually doing it. It is not enough to have good intentions and feelings unless we are able to act upon them.

TO KNOW AND NOT TO DO IS NOT TO KNOW.

A second misconception is that wisdom comes with age and time. Many of us have a picture in our minds of a wise old man with a beard, Gandalf-like, imparting sage-like advice and insight about every challenge or predicament. Or maybe the Zen-like calm of Yoda from *Star Wars*, with his thousands of years of experience.

While wisdom certainly takes time to develop, simple observation shows it takes more than simply growing older to acquire more wisdom. It is sobering to realise that no one becomes wise by simply accumulating knowledge or information over time. Paradoxically while many people fail to become wise as they age, the nature of wisdom is that it is not possible to become wiser except through getting older over the passage of time. While wisdom comes from experience, it doesn't necessarily follow that experience leads to wisdom. The distinction is that wisdom needs experience to be evaluated. It's only when you reflect on what you thought would happen and compare that with what actually happened that you take the first steps along the path of wisdom.

The third myth is that by living in wisdom everything will go well according to our plans or ideas. There is no straight path of uninterrupted progress, accomplishment or success. (We'll see something like that in the life of Job in the next chapter.) Wisdom is not about a problem-free or stress-free life with no mistakes, and it's not about a life with no problems or difficulties. Nor is wisdom only for the super clever. I have been struck by how intelligence, in its common understanding of qualifications and academic knowledge, does not necessarily correlate with success and accomplishment in the outside world. There are numerous accounts of people who did well academically at school then struggled to get anywhere once they left the protection of the academic world. I am one of them. At the same time, there are also many stories of those who struggled at school and went on to become remarkably successful and fulfilled once they developed the rest of their lives. For them, Mark Twain's 'I never let school interfere with my education,' rings true. [131]

The opposite is also true. Being greatly successful in one area of life, for example business, politics or sports, does not mean necessarily that we are living our overall life in wisdom. Francis Chan once said, "Our greatest fear should not be of failure but of succeeding at things in life that don't really matter".[132] One particularly sobering example is the tenth century BC Biblical character Solomon. You may recall from earlier that he has been described as one of the wisest men who ever lived. In the Book of Proverbs, largely written by himself, he wrote,

> *Choose my instruction instead of silver, knowledge rather than choice gold, for wisdom is more precious than rubies, and nothing you desire can compare with her.* (Proverbs ch 8 v10–11)

This exuberant praise of wisdom comes from a man with an annual income of more than $50 million in today's terms! His father, King David, was regarded as the greatest king in Israel's history. Solomon inherited a massive fortune from his father. He was also blessed by God at the start of his kingship. In the Bible (First Book of Kings ch3 v5–14) we read how God appeared to Solomon in a dream. He was probably only in his early teenage years when God offered him anything he wanted. Solomon's response was one of genuine humility. He asked for 'a discerning heart to govern your people and to distinguish between right and wrong'.

God's reply was one of extravagant generosity:

> *Since you have asked for this and not for long life or wealth for yourself, nor have asked for the death of your enemies but for discernment in administering justice, I will do what you have asked. I will give you a wise and discerning heart, so that there will never have been anyone like you, nor will there ever be. Moreover, I will give you what you have not asked for—both wealth and honour—so that in your lifetime you will have no equal among kings. And if you walk in obedience to me and keep my decrees and commands as David your father did, I will give you a long life.*

Yet, in spite of all his wealth and wisdom, Solomon made some very significant misjudgements and mistakes in his own life, leading to a tragic overall evaluation by God.

As an Israelite king, he would have been well aware of the instructions given to kings in the Book of Deuteronomy

This included:

> *The king, moreover, must not acquire great numbers of horses for himself or make the people return to Egypt to get more of them, for the LORD has told you, 'You are not to go back that way again'. He*

> *must not take many wives, or his heart will be led astray. He must not accumulate large amounts of silver and gold.* (Deuteronomy ch17 v14–20)

In spite of these clear instructions, Solomon failed to obey in three significant areas. First, in direct contradiction of being told to not go to Egypt to get horses for himself, he imported 12,000 of these animals (1 Kings ch 4 v26 and ch10 v29). Horses were a sign of enormous opulence and wealth, like the limousines or private jets of today. Second, as if that wasn't enough, he amassed vast amounts of silver and gold for himself from the treasuries of kings and provinces (Ecclesiastes ch 2 v8). Third, he allowed himself to be enticed by many beautiful women who turned his heart astray (1 Kings ch 11 v1–6).

For someone who started with so much promise and potential, that's such a tragic way to end. The sad verdict on his life by God is of one who had done evil! (1 Kings 11ch 6).

My friend Howard Dayton has done an exhaustive study of all the characters in the Bible. Apparently, this amounts to 2,930 individuals. We know in detail about the lives of approximately 100. Of that 100, only about one-third finish well. Of the two-thirds whose lives do not finish well, most fail in the second half of life. Even with all the blessing and encouragement of God, it would seem easy to fall away and lose so much of what He has blessed us with.

If that is the case, why bother with wisdom at all? Because it will lead to enduring and lasting success. Wisdom is what will bring security to those nagging questions at the back of our minds which we mentioned earlier:

1. If we are going to be a person we can live with, what kind of person are we going to be? (*Being*)

2. How do we relate to others in an appropriate way? To my family, my friends, my work colleagues, those who come into my social orbit and the wider global village of which we are all a part. Where do we find the balance between a sober seriousness and appreciating the fun in life? (*Relating*)

3. If we are going to do something meaningful with our life, what kind of work should we do? (*Doing*)

4. Finally, when our life comes towards an end, what do we want our legacy to be? *(Leaving)*

I think we would be hard-pressed to find anyone who would not want to have solid answers to every one of those questions. The challenge is that there are many different paths promising us ways to get there. We all have ideas and assumptions in our minds as to what the best way to get there would be. Although we like to think of ourselves as objective and rational, the reality is that we are much more driven by our emotions than by what we give ourselves credit for. Many centuries ago, theologian Thomas Cranmer expressed it as 'what the heart loves, the will chooses and the mind justifies'.[133] While walking in wisdom is about living life a day at a time, the bigger question is 'where are we heading?' What is the goal we are aiming for? In Western society, it tends to be a journey to find authenticity—to find our true self and express that as fully as we can. In many ways, that's a good thing. However, the problem is that it attempts to place us at the centre of everything. We become the judge and arbiter of what is right—we're the one who decides what wisdom is and what it is not. The reality is that wisdom cannot begin with us. It has to begin with a supernatural and infinite reference point—with God Himself. As I said earlier, this is not a God of our imagination or wishful thinking, but the God of the universe.

We need a map we can trust and rely on. It will come as no surprise that my conclusion is that the best foundation for a life map is the Biblical Scripture comprising the Old and the New Testaments. Based on this, I apply these ancient truths and principles to our modern lives.

The other distinction to make with wisdom is that it is not the same as moral goodness. It may be closely related, but it is not the same thing. There are indeed skills and principles linked to wisdom, but many aspects of wisdom are distinct from the sense of right and wrong. That wonderful source of insight The Book of Proverbs says:

> 'Lazy hands make for poverty, but diligent hands bring wealth.' (ch10 v4)
>
> 'From the fruit of their lips people are filled with good things and the work of their hands brings them reward.' (ch12 v14)
>
> 'The faithless will be fully repaid for their ways, and the good rewarded for theirs.' (ch14 v14)
>
> 'All hard work brings a profit, but mere talk leads only to poverty.' (ch14 v23)

Such proverbs indicate there isn't necessarily a moral dimension to wisdom. Their insight is what is known as 'common grace', available to everyone regardless of what they believe about God.

Wisdom is also not simply a technique or formula for making the right decision in a complex situation. We looked earlier at how wisdom is the ability to unravel the complexities of life when the rules no longer seem to help.

As we go on this quest for wisdom and look at the examples of lives given to us in the Biblical Scriptures, it's striking how full of imperfections and idiosyncrasies they are. They are disappointingly non-heroic. We have just seen that in the life of Solomon and there are countless other Biblical examples.

I remember how I realised this for the first time on my own spiritual quest in my late teens. Until then I had known religious leaders who appeared brave and courageous. The admonition, both direct and indirect, was to be exactly like them. Yet in my own heart I knew that I could never match up to who they were. I knew too well how much fear, worry, self-doubt, insecurity and cowardice lurked deep within me. Up to a point I could present a confident external mask, but inside I felt very different. It's one of the reasons I lost so much hair in my teens!

Compare that to the characters in the Bible. Abraham, for example, is revered not only in the Christian faith but also by

Jews and Muslims—by over a billion people. Less talked about is that when Abraham escaped a famine travelling to Egypt with his wife Sarah, he lied to the Pharaoh about Sarah, claiming she was his sister.

Or Jacob, another widely revered historical figure. This is the same Jacob who cheated his brother out of his birthright and also deceived his father. Moses committed murder and when chosen by God to lead the Israelites out of slavery, he complained about his inadequacy. King David was guilty of adultery and then murder in order to cover up his wrongdoing. In the New Testament, the apostle Peter denied he knew Jesus not once but three times.

It is not their worthiness or merit that is striking. Rather it is, as Eugene Peterson puts it:

> *The intensity with which they live Godwards, the thoroughness in which all the details of their lives are included in God's word to them, in God's action in them. It is these persons, who are conscious of participating in what God is saying and doing, who are most human, most alive.*[134]

By directing our lives towards God, we become more alive and more human. Who would not want that? Yet we turn away. There's something in our human nature that does not want to listen to or follow God's direction. Even after following Christ for over thirty years, I can still see this inclination within me.

The truth is that we do our best to avoid God and would prefer to go our own way. C. S. Lewis picked up on this point around the time a Russian cosmonaut went into space and said he could find no sign of God. Lewis's perceptive response was that understanding how to seek and know God requires a level of thinking different to what we are ordinarily used to. The analogy he gives is that looking for God by exploring the vast universe is like reading all of Shakespeare's plays in the hope of finding Shakespeare as one of the characters. What that means is that for God to exist, He would be related to the universe more as an author is related to a play than as one object in the universe is related to another. As the original Creator, He would have to be outside the order He had created. For this to be the case, how could we either reach him or even avoid Him?

C. S. Lewis's reply is a perceptive and penetrating insight on our age:

> *The avoiding, in many times and places, has proved so difficult that a very large part of the human race failed to achieve it. But in our own time and place, it is extremely easy.*
>
> *Avoid silence, avoid solitude, avoid any train of thought that leads off the beaten track. Concentrate on money, sex, status, health and (above all) on your own grievances. Keep your radio on. Live in a crowd. Use plenty of sedation. If you must read books, select them very carefully. But you'd be safer to stick to the papers. You'll find the advertisements helpful; especially those with a sexy or snobbish appeal.*[135]

The challenge for us in reading such a quote is it goes against the grain of what is popular thinking in general culture and the media—and that is essentially the same wherever you look in the world.

Much of popular thinking is often shallow and opposed to asking the questions that really matter. It requires deliberate effort and choice to decide how to think and look at life and the challenges before us.

In the Sermon on the Mount, Jesus Himself talks of a broad way that leads to destruction and a narrow way that leads to life. The broad way is the popular path that appears easy and relaxed, yet its destination is one of ultimate pain and disappointment. In contrast, the harder, less popular way of self-denial and personal discipline is the way that leads to ultimate life and abundance.

It takes a concerted effort to stand aside from all that is going on around us to seek answers to the really important issues of life—Why am I here, and Do I matter?

These questions become increasingly significant in a world that is rapidly changing in fundamental and important ways. Challenging our assumptions is essential if we are going to be able to grow in wisdom.

REVIEW QUESTIONS TO CONSIDER

1. How much have I allowed myself to believe the myths that wisdom is simply common sense, comes with age, or will guarantee a trouble-free life?
2. What myths about wisdom will I commit myself to exploring?
3. What have I learned from the life of Solomon?
4. What lasting success do I think that wisdom will bring me?

PART 3

DEEPENING IN WISDOM

Live Life in Crescendo! Your Most Important Work Is Always Ahead Of You.

—Personal Motto of Stephen R. Covey

7

DEFINING WISDOM WITH THE DIVINE

I sometimes wish I hadn't delved into the world of religion in the first place, I'm constantly aware that a Higher Being MIGHT be watching my every thought, word, deed, which can be annoying, have we no privacy! I'm not suggesting I'd like to behave however I would like without impunity in a nihilistic fashion, but I'm human and can't be perfect. I do try to do tiny good deeds here and there, not just because it's nice to help someone, but also I hope that some karmic force might hopefully reward me for my good deeds, sound[s] selfish but I'm hoping it's the law of the universe! Whenever I see people who have never set foot in church being blessed, it does make me wonder, 'why should I bother?'

—Comment from Karl to blog post 'Why I Struggle with Religion' on drsunil.com

Having established that we need wisdom, what do we actually mean by this word?

It's a remarkably rich concept and not easy to summarise. Before I lay out some thoughts and principles, it's important we continue to reflect on the sacredness of the subject we are exploring. This is much more than simply making better decisions or getting what we think is best for us. Understanding wisdom in all its richness gets to the heart of what it means to be human. It is as intense as thinking about the wonder of a baby's birth. While the physiological and genetic details of birth are well understood and documented, a scientific approach does not account for the wonder of bringing a new life into the world. I remember as a medical student witnessing a birth. On one level, this was another of the 130 million born every year into the world. But for me, as a raw eighteen-year-old, it was a profoundly reverent experience. As the writer Eugene Peterson put it:

> *In the presence of birth we are at the source of life . . . Here is a mystery, but a mystery of light, not darkness, full of goodness, brimming with blessing. Every birth powerfully recalls us to this source: we have our origins in someone other than ourselves, and greater than ourselves.*[136]

There is something of this awe and wonder when we approach the subject of wisdom. It is wisdom that enables us to realise and appreciate we are far more than our own existence and the narrow world we live in with our preoccupations, doubts, fears, insecurities and often petty concerns.

In seeking to understand wisdom, we need to pause and consider how the process of asking deep questions about life and where we are going takes us to the core of who we are and what it means to be human. We can talk about wisdom in practical, even routine, terms to find answers for complex situations and challenges. That is undoubtedly important. More profoundly, setting out and walking along the path of wisdom is a sacred journey. It is a quest, with all its intensity—a long search for something that is difficult to find. On a quest, the process of transformation is at least as important, maybe more so, than the destination we're trying to reach. This is dramatically out of keeping with our age and the mindset of those around us. As a society we seek a quick fix for problems and challenges before returning to living life on our terms and in our way. As we penetrate into the deeper fullness of wisdom we enter onto holy ground.

We encounter God. Not a god of our convenience or that measures up to the best parts of who we aspire to be, but as the One who is more in control than we are and sees way beyond what we can see. C. S. Lewis expands on this by comparing the Biblical God with pantheism, the belief that God is within everything as opposed to being distinct and separate from His creation. He makes the case for how we oscillate between the idea of God as a harsh, impersonal judge and that of a distant abstract figure neither doing anything in the world nor expecting anything from us in return. We relate to such a God on our own terms at our convenience, in a similar way that we relate to a book on the shelf that we might consider reading at a time that suits us. Such a passive view of God comes naturally to us. But why?

Often in life, we are taken by surprise. In a dark corridor we sense the presence of someone unseen, or during a walk in the woods what seemed to be a lifeless stick turns out to be a living creature. As Lewis writes:

> *An 'impersonal God'—well and good. A subjective God of beauty, truth and goodness, inside our own heads—better still. A formless life-force surging through us, a vast power, which we can tap—best of all. But God Himself, alive, pulling at the other end of the cord, perhaps approaching at an infinite speed, the hunter, king, husband—that is quite another matter.*

> *There comes a moment when the children who have been playing at burglars hush suddenly: was that a real footstep in the hall? There comes a moment when people who have been dabbling in religion ('Man's search for God!') suddenly draw back. Supposing we really found Him? We never meant it to come to that! Worse still, supposing He had found us?*[137]

Here is something of the majesty and power of the God of the Bible. This is not some domestic pet which we can tame and control. He is certainly not a personal assistant whose role is to pamper and provide us with a comfortable life. He is not some impersonal force which we can simply harness to fulfil our agenda. Rather, He is the One who sees and knows all things, having a claim on our lives and pursuing us individually with a passion greater than any human lover ever could. It is in our confusion, maybe even brokenness, that we feel the need to cry out for the wisdom to know which way to turn. In doing so, we discover there is far more there than we had bargained for.

Sudden tragedy or disaster confronts us with our weakness and frailty. But more than anything that is a reminder of our true natural state—we are nowhere near as powerful as we like to imagine ourselves to be. Could there really be someone who holds all this conflicting and contradictory world together and who has the wisdom to make sense of it all?

At this point, if you are of a different religious tradition or of no faith at all, I want to not lose you. I would encourage you to ask the question: Where do you turn when you are at the end of your own resources and there seems no human source of help? Regardless of whom we are and what we profess to believe, all of us are on a search for a fulfilled and meaningful life. Because of our limitations as humans, a life which embraces wisdom has to include the supernatural. That ultimately can lead us only to God. This is God in the fullest sense of the word—the supreme being of the universe who sees, knows and controls all things—even those things and circumstances which from our perspective make no sense to us.

One of the problems we have when we think about God is the image that comes into our minds. For some, it is of a harmless, possibly senile, grandfather sat in the sky who rather vaguely wishes us well. That is very much the pantheist view of God we discussed earlier. For others, their vision is defined by anger at a vindictive person who allows suffering and may even take pleasure in deliberately harming or abusing others. This harsh characterisation has become a popular perspective in secular Western-style societies.

According to atheist Richard Dawkins,

> *The God of the Old Testament is arguably the most unpleasant character in all fiction: jealous and proud of it; a petty, unjust, unforgiving control-freak; a vindictive, bloodthirsty ethnic cleanser, a misogynistic, homophobic, racist, infanticidal, genocidal, filiacidal, pestilential, megalomaniacal, sadomasochistic, capriciously malevolent bully.*[138]

Dawkins' language is one of anger and entrenched hostility. He may have experienced much in the way of hypocrisy and evil from religious people. There has certainly been much of that over the centuries, indeed right up to the present day. I don't know Richard Dawkins' personal experience. But I'm reminded of the words of Blaise Pascal that 'men never do evil so completely as when they do it from a religious conviction'.[139] Terrible evil has been done over the centuries by those who feel they are carrying out God's will. It is also important to remember the great evil that has been done by some of those with an atheistic worldview in North Korea, China and the former Soviet Union. It is strange the number of atheists who, in their anger against faith in God and the evil done in the name of religion, are curiously silent on the subject of evil done in the name of atheism.

I certainly wouldn't want to believe in the kind of God which atheists like Dawkins describe vehemently and scathingly. Nor is this the kind of God that I would want to have anything to do with. But this is not the kind of God who comes through to me when I read the pages of the Old and New Testament.

On my own personal quest for God, I realise that He holds the key to everything that I long and hunger for. A hymn by Timothy Dudley Smith captures this beautifully for me. Although I came across it many years ago, I have hardly ever heard it sung. I find the words profoundly meaningful, even though I am myself a poor singer. The words are worth pondering over, slowly:

As water to the thirsty,
as beauty to the eyes,
as strength that follows weakness,
as truth instead of lies,
as song-time and springtime
and summertime to be,
so is my Lord,
my living Lord,
so is my Lord to me.

Like calm in place of clamour,
like peace that follows pain,
like meeting after passing,
like sunshine after rain,
like moonlight and starlight
and sunlight on the sea,
so is my Lord,
my living Lord,
so is my Lord to me.

As sleep that follows fever,
as gold instead of grey,
as freedom after bondage,
as sunrise to the day,

as home to the traveller
and all we long to see,
so is my Lord,
my living Lord,
so is my Lord to me.[140]

This is the God who is the source and fulfilment of all our longings and desires; the One who can satisfy our heart. In following the simple and everyday longings for refreshing water, for beauty or sleep, we begin to yearn for something richer and deeper. When we feel the aches and longings from the disappointments of life and dreams which have been dashed, we can believe that there is something that will give us the rest that we all long for.

We all do this with an object or an idea. We find something which is beautiful or satisfying in itself and not for what we can get out of it.

Is there a type of music that gives you deep joy? Is there a place, a view or a landscape that evokes the same emotions within you? If someone were to ask you, 'What is the point of that?', would your response be that the music or landscape is not a means to some other end but is deeply satisfying just in itself? My own experience has been that the deepest fulfilment and peace is found in an intimate relationship and communion with the living God.

King David, the father of Solomon, echoed this:

One thing I ask from the LORD, this only do I seek: that I may dwell in the house of the LORD all the days of my life, to gaze on the beauty of the LORD and to seek him in his temple. (Psalm 27 v4)

When we gaze at an object, we do not simply glimpse at it for a moment. We allow ourselves to focus for a sustained period. Instead of asking God for things, we praise, admire and enjoy God simply for who He is. King David doesn't only find God useful in getting what He wants, but He finds God beautiful in Himself. When you're able to sense the beauty of God in your heart, you can experience such pleasure in Him that you can rest content. This is the God we are talking about on the subject of wisdom. The One who knows everything is the source of everything good and beautiful that we see, and the One who understands and holds all of eternity. For me, such a God is worthy of my complete devotion and allegiance. Brad Price puts it this way:

> *To know the will of God is the greatest knowledge,*
> *to find the will of God is the greatest discovery,*
> *to do the will of God is the greatest achievement.*[141]

My experience has culminated in understanding what God says about the subject of wisdom through the Bible. I know of no other book which covers this subject so comprehensively. It captures both the mystery of making sense of life in a complex and changing world as well as offering the clarity of timeless and constant principles to explain wisdom itself.

The Bible ties together closely a proper fear of God with awe and wonder at the Word in the Biblical Scripture. Thus, King David can say 'My flesh trembles in fear of you; I stand in awe of your laws' (Psalm 119, v120). So, for David, there is awe before the Word of God itself as he grasps something of its greatness, coherence and wisdom. This leads directly to the fear of God in terms of the deep, trembling joy and wonder that increases as we relate to Him, not as we imagine Him to be (like the pantheist God we talked about earlier) but as He truly is. The revelation of God through the Biblical Scripture is the only way I can be sure I'm encountering the real God and not a God of my imagination or wishful thinking. It is this Biblical Scripture that becomes the most direct way in which God presents Himself to us, so we can both know Him and remain in faithful relationship with Him.

Hence, we can say that the wise person is not the person who knows the right answers, but the one who has developed the correct responses and relationships to, firstly, God and, in turn, to other people. As such a person becomes deeply based in reality, they understand how the world works. They are familiar with patience and love, listening and grace, adoration and with beauty. This nurtures an ability to see other people as awesome creatures, who are to be respected and befriended, especially those from whom they will derive no benefit in return. At the root of this ability is God as an ever-present centre and an all-encompassing love. Through the power of God working in their lives, they are able to find the motivation, the power and ability to do what they have been called to do in a way that enriches and enhances their relationships.

The Biblical book most directly addressing wisdom is the Book of Proverbs. This is an extraordinary collection of over a thousand wise sayings, often of two poetic lines, each arranged over thirty-one chapters and attributed to Solomon, the son of David, King of Israel. Right at the beginning is a clear understanding of why they are written:

> *Their purpose is to teach people wisdom and discipline,*
> *to help them understand the insights of the wise.*
> *Their purpose is to teach people disciplined and successful lives, to help them do what is right, just and fair.*
> *These proverbs will give insight to the simple, knowledge and discretion to the young.*
> *Let the wise listen to these proverbs and become even wiser.*
> *Let those with understanding receive guidance by exploring the meaning in these proverbs and parables, the words of the wise and their riddles.*
> *Fear of the Lord is the foundation of true knowledge,*
> *but fools despise wisdom and discipline.*
> *(Proverbs ch 1 v2–7, New Living Translation)*

The most important reason why the Book of Proverbs was written was to teach wisdom as a practical life skill. It's the knowledge that helps someone learn to act and to speak in widely different situations. Wisdom includes both the ability to avoid problems and the skill to handle them when they do present themselves. It includes the ability to interpret other people's speech and how to react correctly to what they're saying to us.

How does this help us? Let's say we receive an email that upsets or even angers us. Should we respond immediately by email, should we wait for a day or two or should we get on the phone and talk? Should we do this today, tomorrow or next week? Maybe it would be best to have a face-to-face meeting. What is the best thing to do? We need guidance, from wisdom.

Another everyday example is speaking to someone about an issue that is sensitive and could cause offence or a negative reaction. We know we need to be truthful and to be caring; we know we need to be accurate. All well and good, but how easy is it to get the balance right?

Wisdom gives us the ability to know what we should do and the ability to actually do it.

It's important to grasp that wisdom is much more than intelligence. It does not exclude intelligence, but that is not its main focus. A fascinating part of the Book of Proverbs attributes wisdom to a group of animals not because they have great intelligence but because they know how to navigate life well:

> *There are four things on earth that are small but essentially wise:*
> *Ants—they aren't strong, but they store up food all summer.*
> *Rock badgers—they aren't powerful, but they make their homes among the rocks.*
> *Locusts—they have no king, but they march in formation.*
> *Lizards—they are easy to catch, but they are found even in king's palaces.*
> *(Proverbs 30:24–28, NLT)*

We would not call these animals anywhere near being intelligent by human standards. Yet, they have a remarkable skill at living. Is that not 'wise'?

WISDOM AND HUMAN INTELLIGENCE

Over the last hundred years or so we have measured human intelligence using IQ (Intelligent Quotient) testing. I used these tests while working as a psychiatrist in the field of learning disabilities within the British National Health Service. An important requirement for eligibility to our specialised service is for a person to have a low IQ, below seventy. With an average IQ rated at 100, the higher the number the more intelligent a person is considered. There is even a society, Mensa, for people with a high IQ. People with these higher IQs may have a wide knowledge and often have good mathematical ability. They have greater ability to reason and use logic. But it is fascinating how often there is little correlation between this form of intelligence, character development and future life outcomes.

Excerpts from school reports illustrate this well. These were recorded by Luke Layfield in *The Guardian* on 11 January 2005:

Adolf Hitler (when aged sixteen):

From his secondary-school report card, September 16, 1905: 'Moral conduct, very satisfactory; diligence, irregular; religious instruction, adequate . . . freehand drawing, good; gymnastics, excellent.'

Albert Einstein (when aged sixteen):

His Munich schoolmaster wrote in Albert Einstein's school report in 1895, 'He will never amount to anything'.

Peter Ustinov (actor, filmmaker, theatre and opera director, stage designer, author, screenwriter, comedian, humorist):

'Peter tends to set himself very low targets which he then fails to achieve.'

Gary Lineker (England footballer regarded as one of the country's best-ever players and who has gone on to become a high-earning TV football presenter):

'He must devote less of his time to sport if he wants to be a success.'

'His academic work is handicapped by excessive juvenility. It is time he worked out seriously his objectives in life.'

'Too interested in sport. You can't make a living out of football.'

Paddy Ashdown (British diplomat and politician, fluent in six languages):

'This boy will never learn languages.'

Charlotte Brontë (novelist and author of *Jane Eyre*):

School report said that she 'writes indifferently' and 'knows nothing of grammar'.

John Lennon (musician, singer, songwriter and founder member of the Beatles, the most commercially successful and critically acclaimed band in the history of popular music):

'Hopeless. Rather a clown in class. He is just wasting other pupils' time. Certainly on the road to failure.'

Cilla Black (English singer, actress, entertainer and media personality, who in 2004 was the highest paid female performer on British television):

'Priscilla is suitable for office work.'

Jon Snow (longest running presenter of Channel 4 News):

'Snow has set himself low standards which he has failed to come up to.'

Tim Henman (who, in 2004, reached the ranking of number four in the world at tennis):

A school report said that while he was 'well-balanced, open and friendly,' he lacked the 'killer instinct' expected of a champion.

Alan Sugar, 1960 (business magnate, media personality and political advisor with an estimated fortune in 2011 of £770 million):

'Alan can do better than this. He has ability, but seems afraid to use it.'

It is easy to miss the potential of people by labelling them. While the people in these school reports did not appear to have the conventional intelligence measured or observed by the school system, they had another form of intelligence—wisdom—that enabled them to thrive and develop beyond the classroom.

Emotional intelligence is very close to this concept of wisdom. Daniel Goleman, who has popularised the concept, talks about it as the ability to manage oneself and to manage one's relationships. In 350 BC, the Greek philosopher Aristotle said, 'Anyone can become angry—that is easy. But to be angry with the right person to the right degree, at the right time for the right purpose, and in the right way—that is not easy'.

I am sure that we can all identify with this.

In the 20th century, a different type of wisdom was developed through Daniel Goleman's writing about the idea of emotional intelligence. He describes this form of intelligence as

'the capacity for recognising our own feelings and those of others, for motivating ourselves and for managing emotions well in ourselves and in our relationships'.[142]

While I think this is a very helpful definition of wisdom, I find it lacking. It is too human focussed. It makes an unspoken assumption that we are the beginning and the end of our existence.

My own conclusion is that wisdom comes from being in a reverential relationship with the covenantal living Lord of the universe. It is in Him (with a capital H) that we find the pattern, the path and the power for the well lived life.

Why should that be?

Because He (as God with a capital G) is the ultimate Creator of all, who else could better know how this universe functions best than the One who created it? Who else could know how people best function than the One who created them? As the One who, with such precision and skill, knit us together in the darkness of our mother's wombs, how could He not be aware of every thought, word and action, seen or unseen? Where else could be a better place to go for direction and guidance in life? The Book of Proverbs, again, says:

> *Indeed, if you call out for insight and cry out for understanding, and if you look for it as for silver and search for it as for hidden treasure, then you will understand the fear of the LORD and find the knowledge of God. For the LORD gives wisdom, from His mouth comes knowledge and understanding.* (Proverbs 2:3–6)

The point is clear. If you go looking for wisdom, you'll end up contemplating God. And if you look to God, He will give you true wisdom. That's why we approach this subject of wisdom with awe and reverence.

WISDOM IN THE BIBLE

Three main books in the Hebrew Old Testament are referred to as the Wisdom Literature. These are the books of Job, Proverbs and Ecclesiastes. The literary style of each of these three books is very different. Despite this, they all address the same set of questions concerning the kind of world we are living in and what it means to live well in a world of challenges and contradictions. These books are about how to be good at life.

Each of the three books looks at these questions from a different angle so that when considered together, they give a rounded Biblical perspective on what is a good life.

I find it helpful to share the way that the producers of the online *Bible Project* imagine each of these books as a person. Proverbs is characterised as a sharp, bright young teacher. Ecclesiastes is the incisive middle-aged critic, and Job is the seasoned old man who has experienced so much of the good, bad and ugly of life.

I would encourage you to go to the videos on wisdom produced by the authors of the *Bible Project* at https://thebibleproject.com/explore/wisdom-series/.

Proverbs presents us with a brilliant teacher, Lady Wisdom, who is smart and full of insight about a wide range of life's issues relating to work, relationships, sex and spirituality. These insights would be difficult to develop on our own. This teacher would be the perfect friend to have around when you need really specific advice. Proverbs sees what most people don't see. She believes there is an invisible creative force in the universe that is able to guide people and show them how they should live. It is helpful to think of wisdom resembling gravity. In the same way that gravity is not seen but affects everything we do, so does wisdom affect the whole of life.

In the Hebrew language, this invisible force is called *chokma* and is usually translated into English as 'wisdom'.[143] It is an attribute of God which He used when creating the world. *Chokma* is woven into the fabric of all things and how they work. Wherever people are making good, just or wise decisions, they are tapping into this *chokma* force. Whenever someone is making a bad decision, they're working against this *chokma.*

Or, as Proverbs says, '*the waywardness of fools will destroy them, but the one who listens to wisdom lives in security*' (Proverbs ch 1 v32–33), which is an idea that forms a moral law for the universe. No one can escape from this cause-and-effect pattern in which life has consequences. We act, and that action will produce a result. Lady Wisdom calls out across the earth, making herself available to anyone willing to listen and to learn.

> *You're blessed when you meet Lady Wisdom,*
> *when you make friends with Madame Insight.*
> *She's worth far more than money in the bank;*
> *her friendship is better than a big salary.*
> *Her value exceeds all the trappings of wealth;*

nothing you could wish for holds a candle to her.
With one hand she gives long life,
with the other she confers recognition.
Her manner is beautiful,
her life wonderfully complete.
She's the very Tree of Life to those who embrace her.
Hold her tight—and be blessed!
(Proverbs ch3 v13–18, The Message Translation)

The counter to Lady Wisdom is Mistress Folly. Proverbs repeatedly shows the results of following her advice in preference to Lady Wisdom. Here is the summary from Proverbs, which is explored later:

Folly is an unruly woman; she is simple and knows nothing.
She sits at the door of her house, on a seat at the highest point of the city, calling out to those who pass by, who go straight on their way, 'Let all who are simple come to my house!
To those who have no sense she says, 'Stolen water is sweet; food eaten in secret is delicious!' But little do they know that the dead are there, that her guests are deep in the realm of the dead.
(Proverbs ch 9 v13–18)

The second thing Proverbs explains is that we can access and interact with wisdom and use it to make a beautiful life for ourself or others. Like a designer, we can create with *chokma*. In Hebrew *chokma* is not simply intellectual knowledge. The word is also used to describe the skilled artisan who excels at their craft. Think of someone who is skilled at woodworking or stonemasonry. In the same way, we possess *chokma* when we put it to work developing the skill of making a good life. To know something and not be able to do it is really not to know. Wisdom is knowing a skill that we are able to bring to life in the world we live in. What could be more appealing? Let us find some wisdom and get on with our lives!

There is a third vital consideration to factor in beforehand. In Hebrew thought, *chokma* is not some impersonal force, it is an attribute of God Himself. Our journey to becoming wise begins with what Proverbs calls '*fear of the Lord*'. For American theologian and minister Eugene Peterson, fear of the Lord is as central to the beginning of wisdom as the alphabet is to the beginning of reading. Progress in reading is impossible without mastering the alphabet. Nor is growth in wisdom possible without having the foundation of fear of the Lord.

But what do we mean by fear of God?

There is a kind of fear based on dread of punishment. If we don't do what we are told, we will be in serious trouble. The fear we are referring to here is concerned with avoiding anything that may cause grief or dishonour to the person whom we love and deeply respect. This means that there are only two ways of thinking about life. Either God is at the centre of our life or there is something else. There is no neutral ground. If you value God and your relationship with Him the most, then every other thing will be evaluated in light of that. The alternative is to define reality by our relationship to some other thing, such as money, public opinion, our own feelings or human ingenuity. The stark question we all face is "Do I follow this world's wisdom, to understand the world and myself without reference to God, or can I reject that in order to trust God and His word?"

When we make God the One we fear, we can find the capacity to be not intimidated or enticed by the things of this world that offer no comparison to God's goodness, power and glory. This healthy respect for God's definition of good and evil and true wisdom means learning and not crossing appropriate boundary lines. In Proverbs, this is expanded through the book's literally hundreds of wise sayings. We find examples such as:

> *Put God in charge of your work, then what you've planned will take place.* *(ch16 v3, The Message translation)*

> *The faithless will be fully rewarded for their ways and the good man rewarded for his.* (ch 14 v14)

The Book of Proverbs is about how to study, think and learn the practical discipline of centring all our thoughts and actions on God. The book challenges us to consider that there is a great deal more to life than is at first apparent. Proverbs is about how, having put our trust in God, we should live out that faith.

At the same time life is not as straightforward as Proverbs would suggest. Do you recall that we described Proverbs as a bright young teacher? This teacher is passionate about pursuing wisdom as an attribute of God that is woven into reality. She is optimistic that if we use wisdom, we will build a successful life.

However, as we get older and experience more complexity in life, we find that wisdom is not a simple quest. Contradiction, confusion and challenges loom as obstacles. This is the theme of the next book on our journey to wisdom, the Book of Ecclesiastes. Ecclesiastes is personified as a sharp, middle-aged, somewhat cynical critic who challenges the thinking that using wisdom will simply bring you success. Phrases he uses regularly are 'meaningless,' 'chasing after the wind' and 'life under the sun'. Ecclesiastes describes his quest for wisdom as:

> *I applied my mind to study and to explore by wisdom all that is done under the heavens. What a heavy burden God has laid on mankind! I have seen all the things that are done under the sun; all of them are meaningless, a chasing after the wind. What is crooked cannot be straightened; what is lacking cannot be counted. I said to myself, 'Look, I have increased in wisdom more than anyone who has ruled over Jerusalem before me; I have experienced much of wisdom and knowledge'. Then I applied myself to the understanding of wisdom, and also of madness and folly, but I learned that this, too, is a chasing after the wind. For with much wisdom*

> *comes much sorrow; the more knowledge, the more grief.* (Ecclesiastes ch1 v13–18)

The writer of Ecclesiastes, generally believed to be Solomon, cynically describes applying his mind to wisdom and seeking to understand the seen, material world. The phrases 'under the heavens' and 'under the sun' indicate that he is trying to understand the world in terms of itself. Today we would explain this approach as a scientific or secular view; the effort to find a natural, as opposed to supernatural, explanation for everything. But, despite all the writer's resources and expertise, he comes to a dead end. The implication is we cannot fix human problems with mere technology and knowledge. Science is not capable of changing the human heart. We can earnestly and diligently study pressing issues like racism, crime, and poverty; we may even make progress. But as the mindset of our age is that every phenomenon has a natural cause, a technological solution is always doomed to failure because it is out of touch with reality. In Tim Keller's words:

> *There are supernatural, spiritual problems that need supernatural, spiritual remedies. In the end the more we know the more we see how little we know. This can lead to a sense of helplessness—the more knowledge, the more grief. Human reason unaided by God's revelation will never give us the whole picture.*[144]

Ecclesiastes is written in a style in which two voices appear to be speaking. The first is the teacher, the voice of the *critic*. This is the main voice in the book and is introduced to us by another voice, that of the *author*. The author collects the words of the critic. At the end of the book the author summarises everything and has the final word. The purpose of Ecclesiastes is to challenge our thinking and assumptions about life. The author and the critic explore three disturbing features of the world we live in. They are so disturbing that our natural instinct is to avoid thinking about them. But to walk in wisdom it is essential that we do so.

The first feature is the relentless progress of time. The critic points out that although generations come and go, the earth has been around long before us and will still be there long after. People from long ago are barely remembered—monuments to the famous of the past have been described as expensive sites for pigeon droppings! All the people yet to come will be forgotten also by those who come after. On a cosmic scale, we are but 'the blink of an eye'. Stars are born, then die and form planets that orbit new stars. Even the planets change, eventually burning up. Against this cosmic backdrop, our entire existence is a tiny moment in time.

This is the critic's second, disturbing observation—we are all going to die. We hate facing it until tragedy strikes, as I experienced with my friend Bunty. The reality is that we humans face the same fate as all other creatures. Death comes to all, righteous or wicked, the good and the bad, those who offer sacrifices to God and those who do not. Our destiny is the same. Despite all the frenetic activity sustaining us in this confusing world, we all, eventually, join the dead. How is that for a depressing thought? But bear with me—it doesn't stop there.

The final disturbing thought for the critic is life's randomness. If you've read Proverbs, that is something of a surprise. In Proverbs life is not seen as random. There is a clear cause-and-effect relationship between doing the right thing and being rewarded. The reality is that life does not always work that way. The critic uncovers a fault in the system. Ecclesiastes calls it Chance:

> *I have seen something else under the sun: The race is not to the swift or the battle to the strong, nor does food come to the wise or wealth to the brilliant or favour to the learned; but time and chance happen to them all.*

Moreover, no-one knows when their hour will come: As fish are caught in a cruel net, or birds are taken in a snare, so people are trapped by evil times that fall unexpectedly upon them.

The point is you cannot really control anything in life; so much is unpredictable. Attempts to master and completely control life are destined to lead to failure. The critic uses a metaphor to bring together these disturbing ideas of the passing of time, death and chance. Nearly forty times he says that all life is *hebel*.[145] This Hebrew word means smoke or vapour. This can be interpreted as life being like smoke. It's both beautiful and mysterious. Life takes one shape and, before you know it, has taken a new shape. Like life, smoke looks solid but if you grab it, you find it slipping through your fingers. And when you are in the thick of it, like being in a fog, it's impossible to see clearly.

Modern English translations of the original Hebrew have lost the metaphor and usually translate *hebel* as 'meaningless'. However the critic is not saying that life has no meaning; rather, that its meaning is never clear. This distinction is important. Like smoke, life can be confusing, disorientating and uncontrollable.

"That is all well and good," you may be thinking, "but what are we supposed to make of all this?" Surprisingly the critic, first of all, acknowledges the perspective of Proverbs. He says that it really is a good idea to learn wisdom and to live in fear of the Lord. Even though it does not guarantee success, he knows that it was still the right thing. The second thing he emphasises is that since we cannot control our life, we should stop trying. Instead, learn to hold things with an open hand because we really have control over only one thing—our attitude towards the present. He tells us to stop worrying and choose to enjoy a good conversation with a friend or the feel of the sun on our face or a good meal with people we care about. Our life centres on the simple things, which include both the good and the bad because both are rich gifts from God.

The piercing insights on life in the Book of Ecclesiastes make it dark and painful in places. That is why the author speaks up at the end of the book. He wants us not to lose hope. He wants to make us humble enough to trust that life has meaning even when we cannot make sense of it. And to remain confident that one day God will clear the *hebel* to bring his justice onto all that we've done. Ecclesiastes finishes with:

> *Now all has been heard; here is the conclusion of the matter:*
> *fear God and keep his commandments, for this is the duty of all mankind.*
> *For God will bring every deed into judgment, including every hidden thing, whether it is good or evil.* (Ecclesiastes ch 12 v13–14)

After his long journey to find meaning in education, employment, enjoyment and enrichment, Ecclesiastes concludes that the only thing that really matters is a life which remembers how one day we will have to account to God for all our choices and decisions. Although this is the God who knows and sees everything, there is still much that is mysterious about life. Why is there so much suffering, cruelty and unfairness? It's a timeless question, one that my friend Karl asked right at the beginning of this chapter.

This brings us to a third voice in what is known as the Bible's Wisdom Literature, the book of Job. The book begins with a strange story taking place supernaturally in a place described as some form of heavenly command centre. God appears with angelic creatures that in the original Hebrew are called 'the sons of God'. God points out Job to his servants emphasising Job's righteousness, devotion and virtue. Then, one of the angelic creatures approaches. He's referred to in the Hebrew as *the Satan*. The word used is a title which literally means *'the one who is opposed'*.[146] Out of all those present, he is the one questioning how God is running the world and he argues that Job might not actually love God.

He makes the accusation that Job is only a good person because God rewards him. If God were to take away all the good things he had given, Job's true nature would be revealed. God agrees to this experiment, allowing Satan to inflict suffering on Job. In a devastating outcome, Job loses everyone and everything about which he cares. It's important to remember that Job, as God himself says, deserves none of this. The remarkable lesson is that amid all the suffering, Job continues praising God. To be more accurate, that is the case for chapters one and two. Job concludes chapter one by saying:

> *'Naked I came from my mother's womb,*
> *and naked I shall depart.*
> *The Lord gave and the Lord has taken away;*
> *may the name of the Lord be praised.'*
> *In all this, Job did not sin by charging God with wrongdoing.* *(Job ch1 v21–22)*

But in chapter three, he reveals his real feelings. Job's deep lament reveals his devastation in a long, elaborate curse on the day that he was born. Having opened his heart, Job explains his deep sense of abandonment and pain. Later, friends of Job visit to offer help but all are convinced that only Job's guilt for some horrible wrongs could justify this terrible suffering.

They know that God is just and, as outlined in the Book of Proverbs, the world is ordered by God's justice and fairness. The sole conclusion is that Job must be getting only what he deserves. For the next thirty-four chapters, these friends and Job talk back and forth in a tense dialogue. Job's friends speculate about why God might have sent such suffering and even make lists of the hypothetical sins which Job must have committed. But, after each accusation, Job defends his innocence.

The disturbing truth is Job is innocent! That is why his emotions are so volatile. At some points he is very confident that God remains wise and just. At other times, Job has terrible anguish and doubts about God's goodness. He even accuses God of being reckless, unfair and corrupt. Job, in his deep turmoil, demands that God appear to explain himself in person. And God does come, arriving in the form of a great storm cloud.

What is fascinating is that God does not give Job a direct answer. He does not, as we might expect, tell Job about the conversation with Satan. Instead, He does something very different. He takes Job on a virtual tour of the universe, showing Job how grand the world is. And He questions Job about how capable he is of running this world or even understanding it for just a day. God shows how much detail there is in the world, through things which we might see every day but really do not understand. The key point is that God does understand. He knows everything, and intimately. God pays attention to the beauty and functioning of the universe in ways that we have not even begun to imagine and in places that we will never see.

God concludes by showing Job two wondrous beasts and proclaims how great they are. God admits that they are dangerous, with the power to kill. His big surprise is to say that they are not evil, because they are a part of His good world. That is all God says to defend Himself! It seems so strange. What is the point of what God has said?

From Job's point of view, it seems that God is not just. But we have to remind ourselves, as Job was reminded, that God's perspective is infinitely bigger than ours. He is interacting dynamically with a whole universe of complexity when He makes decisions. This is what God calls His wisdom.

Job asking God to defend himself is an absurdity. How is it possible for any human being to comprehend this level of complexity? It is like expecting an ant to understand nuclear physics!

Where does all this leave us? For Job, it leaves him in a place of humility. He never learns why he is suffering, yet he is able to live in peace and in fear of the Lord. But that is not the ending. After this suffering and humiliation, God restores to Job double everything which he has lost. This response by God raises more questions. Was God rewarding Job for passing the terrible experiences he went through? That does not make sense because as Job losing everything is not a punishment, nor is getting it back a reward. Why, then, does God restore everything to Job? In His wisdom, God decides to give a gift to Job. While no explanation is given, we do learn that Job is the kind of person for whom, no matter what comes, whether good or bad, he can trust the wisdom of God.

Each of these three books, Proverbs, Ecclesiastes and Job, offer a unique perspective on what it means to walk in wisdom and live the truly good life. With the perspective of all three books together we can truly learn to walk in wisdom and have an appropriate fear of the Lord.

But our pursuit of wisdom leaves us with unanswered questions. There is still mystery surrounding this journey of enquiry; we have to find a way of trusting the process without, yet, having all the answers.

This brings us to a surprising realisation. The fear of the Lord increases the more we experience grace and forgiveness. According to the Book of Psalms,

> *If you, LORD, kept a record of sins, Lord, who could stand? But with you there is forgiveness, so that we can, with reverence, serve you.* (Psalms ch 130 v3–4)

All the advice for daily living assumes a holy God who, despite his impossibly high standards, chooses to rescue us. He rescues us not on the basis of our merit, hard work or goodness but on the basis of grace. 'Grace' means unmerited favour—favour that we do not deserve. The ultimate example is the crucifixion to which Jesus went in our place. The implications of this event are the central point on which Biblical faith rests. Theologian and writer Eugene Peterson describes the crucifixion in *God's Message for Each Day:*

> *The single, overwhelming fact of history is the crucifixion of Jesus Christ. There is no military battle,*

> *no geographical exploration, no scientific discovery, no literary creation, no artistic achievement, no moral heroism that compares with it. It is unique, massive, monumental, unprecedented and unparalleled. The cross of Christ is not a small secret that may or may not get out. The cross of Christ is not a minor incident in the political history of the first century that is a nice illustration of courage. It is the centre. The cross of Christ is the central fact to which all other facts are subordinate.*

The Bible teaches us that Jesus Christ died to take the punishment that we deserve. In this way, both the justice and love of God were satisfied. God's justice is satisfied because wrongdoing demands the guilty are punished. At the same time, God demonstrates His love for us by innocently taking upon himself the punishment that we deserve. As the apostle Paul writes in his Second Letter to the Corinthians, *'God made Him who knew no sin, to become sin for us, that we might become the righteousness of God'* (2 Corinthians 5:21).

Theologians and Bible teachers have thoughtfully explained this over the centuries, and it's something that can take a lifetime to grasp. The death of Christ on the cross is the means by which God takes our wrongdoing and the failures in our living for Him and transfers the punishment we deserve onto Christ. By means of this exchange we are accepted by God as much as God completely accepts Christ. Through the cross, the justice and love of God meet. God demonstrates His love for us by sending Jesus to die for us, and God fulfils His perfect justice by ensuring there is appropriate punishment for our failure to live up to His perfect standards.

An apparently trivial example can illustrate this. If I damage your car, you would have three choices. You could ask me to pay for the damage or you could choose to forgive me and pay for the damage yourself. The third option is invoking our insurance policies and leaving it to the insurance companies to decide who will pay. Someone has to pay for the damage—either I pay for the damage, or you pay, or the insurance companies pay. That is the case for physical damage to a car.

How about the damage we cause one another in our relationships? If someone hurts or betrays us, damage to the relationship is caused. There's a loss of trust and a degree of withdrawal in the relationship. The greater the damage caused, the greater the cost to restore the relationship. For a small matter, a simple 'sorry' may be enough. But the greater the hurt or betrayal, then the more it will cost to bring us back into the relationship. In a similar way, our relationship with God is damaged and broken. Because this relationship is the most fundamental and deepest of all, the consequences are also the most far-reaching. There is a cosmic break which no amount of human work or payment can satisfy. Someone has to pay the price. God chooses to pay the price, but even more than that, through grace, we receive undeserved mercy and favour. When we truly understand grace, there is a profound impact on our mental health and well-being.

The best way to convey this is with another simple story. Let's imagine you come to my house to stay. I have to go out and leave you in charge. When I return, you say to me, 'Sunil, while you were out, someone came to the door with a bill to pay and I paid it'. Now, there is one vital piece of information you are withholding—the amount of the bill. If the bill were £1, it is hardly worth even saying thank you. But imagine that it is £20 billion and you had the resources to pay. How would that make me feel? What would having this exorbitant debt paid do to my mental health and sense of well-being? But it gets even better! Not only do you pay the £20 billion bill, you actually credit my account with a further £20 billion and you buy me a new house! It sounds crazy, even ludicrous.

But it is a small picture of what the Bible seeks to convey about how grace impacts the mental health and life of someone who understands it. And this is more than just about our mental health and well-being—this is about what the crucifixion accomplishes for us.

We can say that we understand intellectually the concept of grace. In reality, the way in which we relate to ourself or others is based much more on performance and proving consciously or unconsciously that we are good enough. If we see someone doing better than ourself, it is easy for us to become jealous or resentful. If we see we are doing better than them, it is easy for us to become proud and feel somehow superior. Neither of these responses is wise. Our inner attitudes reveal whether we are defining ourself and others on the basis of performance or grace.

The best way to cure this is to place ourself and what we do in relation to the magnificence and splendour of the God of the universe. When we do that, we develop a realistic understanding of ourself along with our limitations and potential. Such understanding creates a sense of freedom and lightness about life. We do not have to take ourself so seriously. We can laugh at ourself and, at the same time, be serious about our relationship with God. We will explore this idea in the next chapter.

MEET WISDOM IN PERSON

When it comes to wisdom, God doesn't give us an infallible argument or formula to deal with life's challenges and setbacks. He gives us an impregnable person who can handle any situation, no matter how unexpected or expected, and whether major or minor. Life becomes less about what we know and more about who we know. This is about walking in a relationship with the One who is the ultimate author of history and knows all things. While life may not go the way we expect or want, we can look with confidence to the One who knows all things and ultimately controls all things.

This realisation leads to a staggering conclusion. The wisdom we are called to hunger and thirst for is a person, and that person is Jesus Christ Himself. The One who came as a historical figure to earth

WISDOM ULTIMATELY IS LESS ABOUT WHAT YOU KNOW AND MORE ABOUT WHO YOU KNOW two thousand years ago in order to experience the variety of human existence. He died on a cross and three days later was resurrected from the dead. He is the wisdom we hunger and thirst for!

Author Randy Alcorn brings this all together saying, '*All your life you have been on a treasure hunt. You've been searching for a perfect person and a perfect place. Jesus is that person. Heaven is that place.*'[147]

When this truth grips us to our core, we begin on the path to what in Hebrew is called *shalom*. This is the highest form of mental health and well-being, or flourishing, in every dimension of our life. We begin to delight in God for who He is and what He has done for us in Christ.

REVIEW QUESTIONS TO CONSIDER

1. How much am I able to see wisdom as more than a way out of the problems of life?
2. When am I tempted to see God more as my personal assistant to get my goals rather than the One who has the ultimate fulfilment to all my longings?
3. How do the Bible books of Proverbs, Ecclesiastes and Job give me a more balanced view of wisdom?
4. What is so radical about seeing wisdom as a person?

8
FOUR VITAL QUESTIONS

True wisdom consists principally of two parts: the knowledge of God, and the knowledge of ourselves.

—John Calvin (1509–1564)

How does wisdom equip and empower us to live a life such that we rise above the meaninglessness and mediocrity around us and the different challenges we face? I believe it is by enabling us to answer with confidence four questions. They concern the essence of who we are, how we relate to others, how we do the work we are called to do and, ultimately, the importance of what we leave behind at the end of this life. We, ourselves, are leaving for a future that is the greatest mystery of all but should also be a wonderful fulfilment and culmination of this earthly existence.

The four questions are:

1. Being

If I am going to be a person I can live with, what kind of person will that be?

2. Relating

How do I relate to others – my family, my friends, my work colleagues, those who come into my social orbit and the wider global village? Where do I find the healthy balance between sober seriousness and the fun in life?

3. Doing

If I am to do something meaningful with my life, what kind of work should I do?

4. Leaving

Finally, when my life comes to an end, what do I want my legacy to be?

As we unpack each question, I'm going to explain how they have had an impact on my own quest for wisdom before we move on to what could be the implications for your own life. My intention by giving my own experience is to help you reflect on how your life overlaps with my own. I have to preface this by saying these questions are so broad that any explanation here is going to have to be limited in its scope. However, I trust that it can be a helpful starting point for personal reflections on your own quest.

BEING

The question of Being includes identity but is also much more than that. Being is about who we are in relationship to ourself. This includes our intellectual, emotional, physical and spiritual state. It is closely linked with our identity—the way we look at and understand ourself.

We can think about identity on many different levels. *Who am I?* We can answer that question in an endless variety of ways.

At the time of writing this, I am in my mid-fifties, a bald man who is a husband, father, doctor, psychiatrist and of South Asian origin but brought up in the UK. This summary can only go so far in terms of understanding my identity. The greatest influences on this question of identity comes from our own personality and temperament, along with the influence of parents, roots and our earliest experiences.

Although I was born in India, I came to the UK as a toddler. I initially spoke Hindi. The advice given to parents at the time was to speak to their children only in one language, to avoid hindering their progress and education. Many decades later, we know that this approach is misjudged and unhelpful, but such thinking moulded my early development. I grew up speaking primarily English, forgetting most of my Hindi! When I went to school with mainly other English children, I knew I was different. There was a degree of racist abuse from them that reinforced to me that I was different. I began to question my identity and belonging. To complicate matters further, my parents spoke to each other in Punjabi and to me in English! Punjabi is often regarded as less refined and cultured than Hindi with English being considered to have the highest status and prestige!

As a family we still identified with our North Indian roots. Along with a regular diet of Bollywood Hindi films, I found myself feeling that I belonged more to my Asian origins than my West European English environment. Although I could not fully understand the language, the songs and themes of those Bollywood movies awakened a deep longing and yearning in my heart for something secure, permanent and transcendent. This was an age well before the internet and the communication advances to which we are all accustomed now. The lack of actual engagement with family and friends in India created in my mind a fantasy world of perfection and idealism.

My first visit to India after moving to England was at the age of eight. My heart had always leant towards India. But when I went back for those three months, I felt that I didn't fit in. I neither spoke Hindi well nor did I look Indian. I was told that I appeared to be very English, which created confusion about my identity. When I was in England, India was my home; and when I was in India, England was my home. I was always asking the question, "Who am I?"

As I have grown older and discussed this question of identity with an increasing variety of people, I have learnt that this experience is very common. Even those who have not been immigrants have something about their past that makes them feel different from others. It does not matter whether that difference appears to someone else to be significant or not. What matters is the impact on ourselves. It is similar to a distinction often made about major surgery and minor surgery. Being entirely objective we would classify a heart bypass as major surgery and removal of an ingrowing toenail as minor surgery. But for the patient, any surgery is major surgery because it is our body that is being operated on! Regardless of the apparent seriousness of the experience, it is the depth of impact on our thinking that will affect our personal identity.

A sense of identity is strongly tied to our perceived self-worth. So much of what we base our self-worth on can be taken from us. We tend to base this on performance. For me, as a child and teenager, it came from academic success. When I lost that at medical school by failing exam after exam, I crumbled inside. It forced me to search for an identity I could not lose.

Every human-based identity is temporary. We will eventually retire from our job; our role as a spouse or a parent will one day be rudely interrupted by death—ours or that of our loved ones. The only secure identity comes from the One who is transcendent and outside of time.

The consequence of this search is that the ultimate place in which to seek an unshakeable sense of self-worth is from understanding how deeply we are accepted and loved by God. Amidst all the changes of life, God is the only feature which remains unchanging and constant. When anyone asks me who I am, I can answer, "I am a deeply loved and accepted child of

God". It is less a matter of *who* I am than *whose* I am. While that realisation can be comforting, it's only when we understand the basis for this acceptance that life-transforming change becomes possible.

> MY SENSE OF IDENTITY IS LESS ABOUT *WHO* I AM AND, INSTEAD, IT IS ABOUT *WHOSE* I AM.

How do I get a sense of being a completely accepted and loved child of God? For most of my early life I would have answered this question on the basis of my performance or behaviour. Expressed simply, God loves those who do good and He punishes those who do wrong. The problem with this paradigm, as common and natural as it is to think like this, is the question of how do I define what is good and what is wrong? Do I judge only by the laws of the nation? In part, yes. But those laws are subject to variation. Also, complying with external laws says nothing about where my heart is. It's like insisting that a small child say sorry when they are still angry. One might get a verbal apology, but everything about their body language shows they do not really mean it! I can do any number of apparently good deeds, but my heart can remain filled by feelings of superiority, or jealousy or self-recrimination. It was this realisation that ushered me towards the spiritual quest of my late teens.

Christ Himself expressed this incisively during his famous Sermon on the Mount, as recounted in the Gospel of Matthew. He equated anger with murder and lustful thoughts with adultery:

> *You have heard that it was said to the people long ago, "You shall not murder, and anyone who murders will be subject to judgment". But I tell you that anyone who is angry with a brother or sister will be subject to judgment. Again, anyone who says to a brother or sister, "Raca," is answerable to the court. And anyone who says, "You fool!" will be in danger of the fire of hell.* (Matthew ch 5 v21–22)

Raca was an Aramaic word of contempt, a way of dismissively shunning the other person by indicating that they are of no consequence. Jesus goes beyond the insult to the underlying attitude this reveals. He does the same with lustful thoughts:

> *You have heard that it was said, "You shall not commit adultery". But I tell you that anyone who looks at a woman lustfully has already committed adultery with her in his heart.* (Matthew ch 5 v27–28)

These dauntingly high standards challenge the very thoughts and attitudes of our hearts. While lustful thoughts can be deeply private and personal, Jesus refuses to accept that they are trivial or unimportant. With such standards, it's not enough not to resort to physical acts of violence or adultery. It is what is in the heart that is as important. Setting such standards for performance is exceptionally challenging. Who can claim to be pure and without fault?

What about degrees of goodness, the essence of what can be called religious thinking? It is such a natural way of thinking about life. But it is deeply flawed and rarely questioned or challenged. This bell-shaped curve helps explain varying degrees of goodness:

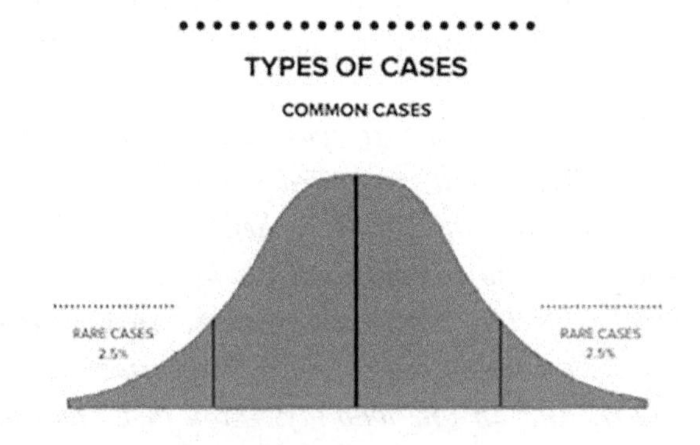

I am not referring to any one religion in particular but to the entire premise behind religious thinking. Whatever our religious background, our professed faith, or even lack of any faith, there's the same premise at the back of our minds.

What is this premise?

It is that God (or the universe or even myself) somehow accepts me on the basis of what I do. By this thinking, the more good I do, the more is God (or the universe or how I feel about myself) likely to accept me. That sounds innocent enough. But it has significant ramifications.

Let me try to explain. If God accepts me on the basis of what I do, what exactly should I be doing and how much doing is good enough? If we think of the above classic bell-shaped distribution curve as a model for goodness with numbers of people on the y-axis and levels of goodness on the x-axis, then we can agree on the outliers—those people who differ very significantly from the mass of our observations. On the one extreme, we have those who most of us would agree were good people—Mother Teresa, Gandhi and Nelson Mandela are obvious examples. At the other end of the curve are those we would generally consider bad—such as Hitler and Stalin.

The rest of us are somewhere in the middle. The problem is that we can only agree on the extremes. But using this paradigm of doing good, where do we draw the line as to who is good? If we arbitrarily say 51% goodness and everyone above that deserves to be accepted, what about the unfortunate person who is only 50% good by their own deeds? And the person who is 52% good. Is it entirely fair that they should be accepted?

Let us take two examples relating to our day to day experience. Driving along the road we go through a red light. The policeman stops us and proceeds to hand out a ticket. Imagine saying, 'Give me a break, police officer! I've been driving for more than thirty years and this is the first time I have gone through a red light!' Could thirty years of faultless driving compensate for one offence?

Or, to be more extreme, let us say we murder someone. Could we make a plea to the judge 'Your honour, I know I did wrong, but I have had problems with anger all my life and this is only the first time that I actually allowed it to get out of control.'?

Could fifty years of no criminal conviction balance out one murder? It doesn't make sense. Religious thinking says that God weighs my good deeds against my bad, and so long as the good balances out the bad, He will accept me. But we know that in everyday life that does not work.

> IF GOD ACCEPTS ME ON THE BASIS OF WHAT I DO, THEN WHAT EXACTLY SHOULD I BE DOING AND HOW MUCH DOING IS GOOD ENOUGH?

In my own personal journey, I've been aware of how much religious thinking permeates me. In my teens, immediately before exams, I would pray much more. It was as if I was trying to prove to God that He should bless my studies because of my level of devotion to Him. In my first year at university, I struggled with questions of identity and belonging that also led to a period of depression. I became acutely aware of how much within me was not right and was dishonouring to God. I could do apparently good things on the outside, but my heart was filled with so much which was flawed that I lacked congruency between the outside and inside. *(For more on this topic see the 15 minute video at drsunil.com/me .)*

The first step has been coming to faith in Christ as the One who has lived the perfect life. Even so, I still find within me a propensity for religious thinking. I know now that I am accepted on the basis of what Christ has done on the cross and not according to my own performance. Despite this powerful realisation, it remains easy for my emotional health to be governed by my own perception of how I am doing. If I perceive myself to be doing well, such as doing the things I need to do or getting appreciation from others, while that can be a good thing, there is a hidden danger. It is easy for that sense of feeling good about how I am doing to cross the line over to a sense of superiority or arrogance with regard to other people. In contrast, when I am struggling to keep up, when I am disappointing others, there is the temptation to go towards despondency or even despair.

But, let us assume that the basis of my acceptance had nothing to do with my performance? What if it were based on the performance of someone who was perfect in every way? What if my acceptance were based on a different life which had been sacrificed for me so I could be right with God? In this case my acceptance comes from trusting someone who has made a path whereby I can come to God; it is based not on my merit but on the merit of Christ.

That is why the cross of Christ and the Gospel are such good news.

I love the simplicity and depth of this old Anglican prayer:

Almighty God, our Heavenly Father,
We have sinned against you and against our neighbour, in thought, word and deed;
Through negligence, through weakness, through our own deliberate fault.
We are truly sorry and repent of all our sins.
For the sake of your Son Jesus Christ, who died for us, forgive us all that is past;
And grant that we may serve you in newness of life, to the glory of your Name.
Amen.

I struggle with religion because it gets in the way of experiencing and knowing how much I am truly loved. Religion puts my own performance ahead of the One who has done everything for me. I need reminding of that every day. A simple daily reminder of that is the four simple questions, and answers, which I aim to repeat to myself each morning. They were first told to me by one of the ministers of our church, Rico Tice. I think they describe an important key to living a life that has a deep sense of belonging and inner security.

***Question 1*: When did God call me to Himself?**

Answer: From Scripture, I learn that it was before the creation of the world. '*For He chose us in Him before the creation of the world to be holy and blameless in His sight'* (Ephesians ch1 v4). What a wonderful sense of security that gives me! My acceptance by God has nothing to do with my merit but everything to do with God's goodness and divine favour.

***Question 2:* What does God think of me right now?**
Answer: God is delighted in me right now because He looks at me the same way that He looks at Jesus—'*God made him who had no sin to be sin for us, so that in him we might become the righteousness of God*' (Second Letter to the Corinthians ch5 v21). This is not about what I do or do not do but what God has already done for me in Christ through crucifixion on the cross. The greatest work is already done, so that I can take on lesser challenges with confidence and joy!

***Question 3*: What kind of day is it going to be today?**
Answer: It's going to be an absolutely wonderful day because there are going to be numerous opportunities to become like Jesus. God will use the temporary problems and afflictions of this life to mould me into someone who can endure into eternity.

***Question 4:* What kind of day is it going to be tomorrow?**
Answer: It's going to be an absolutely wonderful day because I will be one day closer to meeting face-to-face with Jesus, the One who is the source, embodiment and fulfilment of all wisdom and joy!

From these questions and answers can come a great sense of confidence as I acknowledge with gratitude the miracle God has wrought to bring me into a relationship with Him. That means that I do not live *for* approval but *from* approval. The privilege and experience of being saved by grace releases the power for change to come not from my own strength but through God and His eternal word. The single word '*grace*' sums this up. Grace is God's undeserved mercy and favour to those who not only do not deserve it but who should also be punished and condemned. It's such a revolutionary concept. Many believe that if grace is not the most wonderful thing in your life right now, you can be sure that you have not understood it.

UNDERSTANDING GRACE MEANS NOT LIVING *FOR* APPROVAL, BUT *FROM* APPROVAL.

RELATING

Life only makes sense ultimately in relationship to others. The two greatest commandments by my favourite teacher are '*to love God with all your heart, mind, soul and strength*', and '*to love your neighbour as you love yourself*'. It's hard, if not impossible, to come up with anything better than that! Living for myself and my own selfish desires can never be enough. It is good to remember that 'the whole world consists of other people'! How we relate to others tells a lot about ourselves.

The apocryphal story of a wise man travelling between two cities illustrates this. On the way, he meets someone travelling from City A to where this wise man has just been, City B. The traveller asks him, "What are the people in City B like?" His reply is to ask, "What were the people in City A like?". The traveller replies, "Those in City A were nasty, mean, cruel and vindictive". The wise man replies, "Then, that is what the people in City B will be like". A little while later, the wise man meets someone travelling in the opposite direction. He is asked the same question but this time about City A. He asks this second traveller, "What are the people in City B like?" The traveller replies that those in City B are kind, compassionate and honest. You may have deduced that the wise man replies, "That is how you will find the people in City A!"

The parable illustrates one of the surprising generalities in human relationships, that other people can act as mirrors, reflecting the attitude of others. The key with these people is to initiate the attitude that you want to see returned.

On Sundays I attend a large church with my family, All Souls, Langham Place in Central London. I have noticed on a number of occasions how my state of mind affects the quality of conversations with those who are there during coffee time after the service. When I am positive and upbeat, everyone else seems to share this cheerfulness. What is fascinating is how the opposite also happens. When I am less motivated and I feel inward looking, everyone else seems to share what may even lapse into moroseness. Mirroring our state of mind with that of others is a vital skill if we are to develop satisfying and mutually fulfilling relationships.

The great part of our meaning and fulfilment in life comes from the relationships with which we surround ourselves. Early in life, we have limited choices as to who that is with. However, as we grow older, the challenge is to begin questioning the assumptions and worldview that we learned from our past in order to see if they still hold up with the reality developing before us. We begin to learn that not everything that others say can be trusted. This means we have to learn discernment about the motives and intentions of others. We make and break friendships and relationships. Some of this happens because of the pain and hurt we cause each other. At times it can simply be the result of no longer being in physical proximity or because our paths do not cross. We may, and often do, outgrow those relationships as we sense different priorities and ways of looking at life and the world.

Not everyone will stay on the journey with you. It is important to realise that 'that's all right'. I wish I had understood this truth earlier in my life. Many times I have found myself putting too much expectation on the relationships around me and finding myself hurt and disappointed. The challenge is to maintain a tender heart while keeping a tough skin.

My faith journey to Christ brought me into conflict with my immediate family. No matter how hard I tried, it was clear that we were on different wavelengths. This was a particular disappointment for my parents. While I accepted I needed to love and honour them as my parents, I also saw I needed to create an identity elsewhere for my life decisions and community. I became part of a church community that helped me understand and grow in my understanding of Christ. It was also a place from which

I could continue to honour and respect my parents in spite of the clear differences in our faiths. A great bonus of this time was that I met the woman who would eventually become my wife!

For a number of years after my spiritual awakening, I looked up to people who were religious. I admired their dedication to God and their Biblical knowledge. They seemed so strong and sorted out that I wanted to be like them. For many years, I hung around those kinds of people. During that time, I grew a lot and learned a lot about God. But, unknowingly, I also moved progressively further away from being a real person. I became increasingly religious but less of what I now understand to be spiritual. My perspective on that time is that I was actually losing touch with many other aspects of what it means to be human—my vulnerability and pain, my need for other people, my wilfulness and inner darkness. The sudden death of my close friend Bunty was the most traumatic of a number of wake-up calls for me. I had to begin looking at why I couldn't get close to people and trust them at a very deep level, and why I felt further and further away from God no matter how much I understood about Him.

I discovered people with whom I felt safe opening up to about my pain and inadequacies. As I grew closer to others, my vulnerability increased and I needed them more. The safe people around me loved me exactly as I was, and I learned to open up about my struggles, sinfulness and imperfections. I began growing as a person and learned a great deal more about God than I had known when I had been focussed on being religious.

It was from there that I became better able to recognise people who were not authentic even though they seemed very spiritual. I found that I was able to pick better friends—people who really knew God and his ways, instead of those using a great amount of religious language and activities. These were people with a true ability to develop relationships, who were able to understand and love others while being honest about themselves and about life.

Those who are closest to us will have profound implications on our future direction and growth. It's important that if we are committed to our growth and development, that we find what

Henry Cloud calls 'safe people'.[148] Such people help us in three ways. First, they enable us to become more of who we were created to be. Second, they bring us closer to God. Third, they help us to build relations with other people.

So many of our relationships can be merely a transaction. It is so easy to treat others as objects that we use for our own ends and purposes. We forget that inanimate objects are what we *use*, but that we *relate* to human beings. Although in many cases we cannot avoid basing our relationships on a transaction, it's vital to recognise that our fellow human beings are also made in the image of God. This is the case regardless of their gender, race, level of intelligence, religious identity or sexual orientation. Learning to love and accept others for who they are and not only for what we can get out of them is a hallmark of wisdom and a vital human skill.

At the same time, it's vital to recognise that not all relationships are of equal value to us personally. We can only relate meaningfully to a finite number of people. Psychologists talk of Dunbar's Number, a concept developed by British anthroplogist Robin Dunbar which states that the maximum number stable relationships which an individual can maintain is about 150. That does not mean social media should have no place in our lives, but we do need to accept that the number of people with whom we can sustain meaningful relationships is finite.

After my relationship with God must come, in my case, the relationship with my spouse. This comes ahead of that with my children. Indeed, as a husband and father, I value the idea that the best way to love your children is to love their mother. Beyond this close group is my social network, work colleagues, my extended family and friends. How do I view and look at those relationships?

Proverbs talks about this in terms of the righteous and the wicked. When we read such words, we immediately think of those whose lives are moral and those whose lives are immoral. However, that is only a part of the meaning. In the original Hebrew language, the words for righteous (*tzedeq* and *mishpat*) have a strong connotation of relationships.[149] Bruce Waltke, a commentator on Proverbs, wrote, '*The righteous are willing to disadvantage themselves to advantage the community; the wicked are willing to disadvantage the community to advantage themselves*'.[150] So, a righteous person sees everything they have been given, including time, money, resources and social connections, as for the good of those around them. By contrast, the wicked see everything they have as something to be used for their own selfish purposes.

The key difference is seeing that we are accountable in our relationships. The ultimate accountability is to God, who has provided everything for us. When I grasp how much God has secured for me in Christ, I can begin to be at peace with the person He has made me, with both my positive and my negative experiences. This is not a one-time experience but an ongoing and growing realisation, day by day and through even the different seasons of life.

The experience includes learning to forgive others for the way they have disappointed us or let us down. When someone hurts or disappoints us, it's easy either to attack that person or to withdraw from the relationship in a negative way. However, it is only in mathematics that two negatives make a positive. In relationships, reacting negatively to a person who is negative towards us can never be ultimately helpful. Refusing to forgive those who hurt us and holding grudges is like drinking poison and expecting the other person to die. The power of forgiveness brings a well-documented benefit to our emotional and psychological health.

The power to forgive comes from a deepening awareness and understanding of how much we have already been forgiven through Christ. As we grow in awareness and sensitivity to our flaws and weaknesses, we can look with compassion to others who let us down or disappoint us. That is so different from a world where it is easy to condemn and criticise others who we feel are in the wrong. By focusing on the faults of others, repeatedly rehearsing how we have been wronged or betrayed, we play the victim and take the responsibility for change off ourselves and put it onto other people. The tragedy of this way of thinking is the trap of blaming others, wasting time and energy on the hurts of the past. At extreme levels this can lead to hatred and vilification of complete groups of people. The Russian dissident Aleksandr Solzhenitsyn (1918–2008) was sentenced to eight years in a labour camp and then internal exile for criticising Josef Stalin in a private letter. In *The Gulag Archipelago* he wrote:

> *If only there were evil people somewhere insidiously committing evil deeds, and it were necessary only to separate them from the rest of us and destroy them. But the line dividing good and evil cuts through the heart of every human being. And who is willing to destroy a piece of his own heart?*[151]

Maybe this is why we enjoy criticising others so much; we are diverted from looking at our own conflicted and corrupted hearts. It's much easier to talk about the sins and mistakes of others. That raises the question of the terrible evil that is evident in the world around us. We will come to that shortly. But, before we do, let us look at a helpful way to group people as we relate to and interact with them.

Categorising people may seem unduly harsh—especially if there is no self-reflection. However, it is very apparent from both our own experience and the scientific research that not everyone is the same in their outlook on the world. That means we cannot treat all people in the same way. Even though we are all of equal value and worth, everyone differs in what is important to them and how they process life and their experiences. Some of those differences relate to temperament and personality while others relate to deeper aspects of moral values.

John Maxwell's *Law of the Inner Circle* is a good shortcut for deciding who we should spend time and energy with as it forces us to think about our priorities, vision for life and values.[152] His 'law' states that our potential in life is determined by those who are closest to us. This closeness goes way beyond physical proximity to those with whom we feel emotionally connected, as well as those to whom we look, respect or admire.[153] Another way of expressing this is . . . '*who are the travel companions you are bringing along with you on the journey of life?*'. Henry Cloud provides a useful distinction between different kinds of people.[154] The perceptiveness of these distinctions has roots in the timeless wisdom of Biblical Scripture.

As we look at these three types of person—*Wise, Foolish and Evil*—it is worth remembering that elements of all three are in each one of us. We can certainly apply the framework to others. But every one of us, if we are realistic about our own heart, can see aspects of all three within ourselves. The key question is:

What does this person do when truth comes to them?

The Wise Person

When they are confronted with reality, a wise person will adjust themselves to that reality. They are hungry to grow and relish feedback. When we tell them what they're doing wrong or could improve, they welcome the input and make appropriate adjustments. If you have come this far in this book, then you are most likely in this category.

One challenge we are likely to have is to assume that other people are like us. As a result, when we give feedback, we tend to assume they, too, will graciously receive it. People differ radically in the way they respond to the truth. It is easy to be unaware of what we are missing or the assumptions we are making, especially when dealing with what is a blind spot for us. The wise person takes the feedback without feeling personally negative, especially if it is given with love and respect. They learn and grow from this insight. We may even be thanked for a priceless gift!

During 2001–2018 I had junior doctors working with me, usually for six months at a time. Part of my responsibility towards them as my trainee doctors was to give regular feedback. With one particular doctor I had to give some difficult feedback on her communication style. I hesitated about giving it as I was not sure how she would take it. When I did, I was pleasantly surprised by her positive response and strong desire for me to comment on any future occasions when she lapsed into her previous habits.

A mark of a wise person is hunger to learn, grow and develop themselves. The key for us, if we are their leader, is to continue giving feedback and encouragement. As we do that, we will see them grow and flourish. You will also win a friend. '*Do not rebuke mockers or they will hate you; rebuke the wise and they will love you*' (Proverbs ch 9 v8).

The Foolish Person

We have previously looked at how when the Bible uses the word fool, it's not a measure of intelligence or IQ. Such people can be very gifted or talented. They can also be charming and wealthy. What defines them is that when they are forced to confront reality, whether about themselves or their behaviour, they will try to adjust the truth rather than adjust themselves. Typical responses are to ignore the truth, externalise the issues or attack the messenger.

When you confront a fool, you are told quickly that the problem is somewhere else. The Fool rejects all responsibility for their actions. They become defensive and regard you and your feedback with contempt. They may seek to close down the conversation to prevent them having to really listen to the issues.

I remember a colleague I worked with many years ago. He had a tendency to upset people. Initially, I thought that this was the result of a personality clash. Then I noticed how he upset a variety of other people whenever I was not around. People with whom our department had no previous problems were suddenly very upset with us. I talked to this colleague on a number of occasions. Every time he gave me some distracting explanation of why things were the way that they were. Initially, I was sympathetic. Over time, it became apparent that the issue was centred on this particular individual and not other members of the team or the department. Sadly, because he lacked the insight to see the role he played it proved very difficult to help him.

Talking to a wise person leads to improvement in the situation. With a fool, the opposite happens. The more we talk about the issue, the more we realise how little progress we are making. Indeed, the situation may become worse and more complicated.

With a foolish person, there has to come a time when talking stops and they understand about responding to consequences. Only when they feel the pain from their behaviour will they change.

All of us are foolish to some degree or other. The New Testament even teaches us that Jesus died for fools. When dealing with someone behaving in a foolish manner, the challenge is to limit our response just to actions that can no longer be tolerated and ensure that there are consequences if they refuse to change.

The Evil Person

It can sound particularly harsh to describe someone as evil, but this has to be the final verdict on some people, even according to the Bible. The evil person is someone who has destruction in their heart and has decided to inflict pain. Such people are too dangerous to deal with on our own. Rather, we need what Henry Cloud calls 'lawyers, guns and money'.[155] We need protection in some form or other, maybe even by calling the police.

We are told to respond to everyone with love and understanding. Many times that can be very helpful. I have also concluded that such an approach can be deeply flawed and does not face up to some terrible broken corners of our world.

While I would agree with those who say that we need to focus on love and understanding, we also have to engage with the realities of the world around us. As a psychiatrist I have had patients who have done terrible things. They have been treated with great compassion and respect by the Health Service. In some cases, I've seen how even though this support and compassion has been provided over many years, they still continue with their crimes. When I talk to them it becomes clear that some don't want to face the consequences of their actions and, given the opportunity, will revert to their previous behaviour. We spend huge amounts of money protecting the public from them.

The spiritual renewal author Becky Pippert wrote about what kind of God gets angry in *Hope Has Its Reasons: The Search to Satisfy Our Deepest Longings*. She encourages us to think about how we would feel about seeing someone whom we love destroying their life through unwise relationships or actions. If we really cared about that person, we would not just tolerate seeing them harm themselves. We would be deeply moved, even angry enough to help them see the danger of what they are doing. This response shows that the opposite of love is not anger. The true opposite of love is hatred, and the final form of hate is indifference. What that means then, she wrote, is '*God's wrath is not a cranky explosion, but His settled opposition to the cancer . . . which is eating out the insides of the human race He loves with His whole being*'.[156]

As the Bible explains, God's wrath flows from His love and delight in His creation. He is angry at evil and injustice because it destroys peace and integrity. Some people think that believing in a God of judgement leads to more violence—in some places it does. As Tim Keller puts it, '*If you believe in a God who smites evildoers, you may think it perfectly justified to do some of the smiting yourself*'.[157] We have countless examples of people using their belief in God to justify violence around the world.

But interestingly, Miroslav Volf, a Croatian who has seen violence in the Balkans, has a different view of God's judgement. In his book, *Exclusion and Embrace*, he wrote:

> *If God were not angry at injustice and deception and did not make a final end to violence—that God would not be worthy of worship . . . The only means of prohibiting all recourse to violence by ourselves is to insist that violence is legitimate only when it comes from God . . . My thesis that the practice of non-violence requires a belief in divine judgement will be unpopular with many . . . in the West . . . [But] it takes the quiet of a suburban home for the birth of the thesis that human non-violence [results from the belief in] God's refusal to judge.*

> *In a sun-scorched land, soaked in the blood of the innocent, it will invariably die ... [with] other pleasant captivities of the liberal mind.*[158]

Volf's point is that unless we have truly suffered deep injustice and betrayal, it is very hard for us to understand the need for an all-encompassing solution to the horrific pain that others have gone through. Volf is considered radical by modern thinking that doubts God, an approach characteristic of Western secular thought. His conclusion is that by actually removing belief in God, a foundation for even more violence is created. When violently abused, the outcry is to make those who are responsible for the crimes pay in full. How much more so if you have seen your home burned down and your relatives killed and raped. To just say 'violence will not solve anything' is a meaningless platitude that belittles this genuine desire for justice. The problem is that victims of violence can be drawn into a cycle of ever-increasing violence that goes even beyond the original evil. The pain and anger of having one of my eyes pulled out leads me to say, 'I will pull out both of your eyes'. Without an eternal judge to intervene, a cycle of revenge and retribution can never end. That is happening in many parts of the world. Generations of appalling violence have led to a never-ending hunger for yet more violence.

This is a world where it often appears that those who do terrible evil get away with their actions and even seem to prosper in life, dying peacefully in their beds. Modern Western-style secular thinking has no answer to how one responds to appalling injustice that goes unpunished. Is it any wonder that calls for restraint in many parts of the world fall on deaf ears? That leads to the key question . . . 'is there a way for this genuine desire for justice to be honoured in a way that does not lead to this never-ending spiral of more violence?'. For Volf the best resource is belief in the concept of God's divine justice.

Keller concludes:

> *"If I don't believe that there is a God who will eventually put all things right, I will take up the sword and will be sucked into the endless vortex of retaliation. Only if I am sure that there's a God who will right all wrongs and settle all accounts perfectly do I have the power to refrain."*[159]

But for doubting secular Western-style thinking, this approach creates a real dilemma. This thinking has no room for anything beyond the present life. In his essay 'The Discreet Charms of Nihilism', the Nobel Prize-winning Polish American poet Czelaw Milosz updates Marx's description of religion as 'the opium of the people' because the promise of an afterlife led the poor and working class to put up with unjust social conditions.

> *And now we are witnessing a transformation. A true opium of the people is a belief in nothingness after death—the huge solace of thinking that our betrayals, greed, cowardice, murders are not going to be judged ... [but] all religions recognise that our deeds are imperishable.*[160]

Many people complain that belief in a God of judgement will lead to a more brutal society. Milosz has personally seen, in both Nazism and Communism, that a loss of belief in a God of judgement can also lead to extreme brutality. The underlying problem is that if we are free to shape life and morals, whichever we choose, without ultimate accountability it can lead to violence. Both Volf and Milosz conclude that understanding God's final judgement in society is a necessary foundation for human practices of love and peacemaking.

In other words, a truly loving God cannot help but be angry when evil and injustice erupt into a broken world. Understanding that can truly restrain vengeance and further violence.

DOING

This is where it gets even more personally challenging. We can talk about these issues in the abstract sense, but what does it mean for us with this life that we have been given? When we wake up in the morning, there are jobs to do and errands to run. We have responsibilities, but what are we called to do that only we can do? This lack of clarity is especially true in the day-to-day routine of life with the myriad of choices at our disposal.

The early twentieth century American evangelist Dawson Trotman said something that I find an enormous challenge. '*Never do anything that someone else can and will do, when there is so much of importance to be done which others cannot or will not do*'.[161]

There are plenty of good and even noble things that we could do. How do we decide which ones to make our responsibility, guided by the wisdom that 'the best is the enemy of the good'. The key is finding and walking into whatever is our God-given calling. It is important to grasp that this is not a simple one-off process. It will involve experimentation and failure to such an extent that failure is an important part of the process. The American spiritual and community leader Parker Palmer addresses this with his question, '*Is the life I am living the same as the life that wants to live in me?*'[162] We tell ourself this is a path that we want to take, but how many of our choices and decisions come from our ego or desire to impress others? There is a calling within us that we also need to recognise and respond to.

The Bible asserts that God has prepared good work for us to do that is unique to us. '*For we are God's handiwork created in Christ Jesus to do good works which God prepared in advance for us to do*' (Letter to the Ephesians ch 2 v10). The word for handiwork is the same word from which we get the word poem. It is a work of art with God being the master craftsman. It is a reminder of understanding and embracing 'the good works which God prepared in advance for us to do'.The first part of that verse also reminds us that we are 'God's workmanship created in Christ Jesus'. In other words, all our life experiences are going in a certain direction, equipping us for unique tasks and opportunities. The disappointments and struggles we have had can become the training ground for learning how to help others who are going through similar experiences. We can empathise and support them better because we personally know what it's like to experience the same things.

There's a universal deep longing in our hearts for greater meaning and purpose. Our lives can feel ordinary and mediocre, but that's not what we are called to. The danger comes from confusing task with the nature of our sense of identity. What we are doing may not appear to be particularly glamorous or high profile, but that does not take away its intrinsic worth. There is One who sees and knows all.

We all want to have something meaningful to do with lives that can seem rather mundane and ordinary on many levels. Martin Luther King said,

> *If a man is called to be a street sweeper, he should sweep streets even as Michelangelo painted, or Beethoven composed music or Shakespeare wrote poetry. He should sweep streets so well that all the hosts of heaven and earth will pause to say, 'Here lived a great street sweeper who did his job well'.*[163]

When considered like that, there is no work that should be considered minor or trivial when it is done for the One who sees and knows all things. Every day can be a masterpiece. The between-the-Wars English philosopher and Unitarian minister L. P. Jacks wrote:

> *A master in the art of living draws no sharp distinction between his work and his play; his labor and his leisure; his mind and his body; his education and his recreation. He hardly knows which is which. He simply pursues his vision of excellence through whatever he is doing and leaves others to determine whether he is working or playing. To himself, he always appears to be doing both.*[164]

What I love about this description is the way that all life is seen as one complete whole and not a collection of competing or conflicting pursuits.

Our obsession with work and success is one of the great flaws of modern, 21st century life. When we build our identity around our work, if we succeed we are in danger of becoming proud and arrogant; if we do not succeed we risk feeling devastated and sinking into despair.

As discussed earlier, making work the basis of our identity is a form of idolatry. The word 'idol' refers to something that has been elevated to being more important and significant in our life than the God who is the originator and source of the universe and every good thing in the world. Work becomes too important to us and is our ultimate source of security and satisfaction. Work was never meant for that—it is a good thing that risks easily becoming an ultimate thing. We risk attributing to work qualities that are God-like and that only God can ultimately provide.

How can we strike the balance? How can we find joy in what we do without becoming so obsessed that we neglect our health, family, friends and important relationships? How can we avoid feeling paralysed with fear, doubt and even self-loathing when we make a mistake?

The spiritual awakening of John Coltrane, the famous jazz musician, changed his attitude about his work and ability to make music. He realised that before his spiritual awakening, making music was mainly about himself. He made music to make himself feel good about himself. However, once God filled his soul, the music became about other people. Music became a means to serve them.[165]

This insight is liberating by showing that all work, no matter how apparently trivial it may seem, has intrinsic worth and dignity. Work becomes a means of serving and blessing other people in the same way that God seeks to bless and provide for us. Martin Luther uses Psalm 145 to teach that God feeds everyone he has made.[166] How does he feed us? God feeds us through other people's work. The farm girl who milks the cow; the truck driver who delivers the milk; and the storekeeper who sells the milk. All work is God's work, and all work has intrinsic dignity.

We tend to look beyond serving our neighbour to self-advancement for its own sake in order to make ourselves feel better than other people. C. S. Lewis builds on this with:

> *Pride gets no pleasure out of having something, only out of having more of it than the next man. We say people are proud of being rich, or clever, or good-looking, but they are not. They are proud of being richer or cleverer, or better-looking than others. If everyone else became equally rich, or clever, or good-looking there would be nothing to be proud about.*[167]

The result is that pride drives us to take on more work than we should, or to neglect ourselves and our important relationships. Pride can also justify our own laziness!

The song 'Before You I Kneel, My Master and My Maker' by Keith and Kristyn Getty captures the sense of finding the right balance:

> *Before You I kneel, my Master and Maker*
> *To offer the work of my hands.*
> *For this is the day You've given Your servant;*
> *I will rejoice and be glad.*
> *For the strength I have to live and breathe;*
> *For each skill Your grace has given me;*
> *For the needs and opportunities*
> *That will glorify your great name.*
>
> *Before You I kneel and ask for Your goodness*
> *To cover the work of my hands.*
> *For patience and peace to shape all my labor,*
> *Your grace for thorns in my path.*
> *Flow within me like a living stream,*
> *Wear away the stones of pride and greed*

'till Your ways are dwelling deep in me
And a harvest of life is grown.

Before You we kneel, Our Master and Maker;
Establish the work of our hands.
And order our steps to seek first Your kingdom
In every small and great task.
May we live the gospel of Your grace,
Serve Your purpose in our fleeting days,
Then our lives will bring eternal praise
And all glory to Your great Name.[168]

What do I find so personally helpful about this song?

When I start my day, it helps me to remember that what I do is firstly an offering to God. Everything that I do and that I have originates in what God has already done for me. My life is a response to His goodness, love and care—the day that lies before me, the health and strength I enjoy, the skills He has given me and the opportunities to serve Him through other people. I cannot and must not take them for granted as they are all manifestations of His abundant grace.

At the same time, life and work have challenges, problems and difficulties. It is easy to think that a life with no challenges would be better; yet it is just these problems and difficulties that build the qualities of grit and resilience into us. I need, as the second verse of the Getty song describes it, 'patience and peace to shape all my labour'—to prevent frustrations destroying my peace of mind and my security in God's provision. Life may not be going the way that I want; there may be difficult colleagues and challenging situations. All of these are, I believe, a part of God's plan for refining and developing me.

Finally, we want to know that whatever we do has been meaningful and worthwhile. We want to know that however little glamour or drama there may be about what we do, whatever it is has made a difference in some way. We want something meaningful to do with our lives that can, on many levels, seem rather mundane and ordinary. Mother Teresa's powerful quote explains that, 'We may not be able to do great things, but we can do small things with great love'.[169] We can put our whole devotion, energy and passion into the most mundane of tasks. We can sweep streets with the commitment that Michelangelo brought to painting pictures, Beethoven composing music and Shakespeare to writing poetry.

LEAVING

How can we enjoy the journey of our life without regret? Our legacy is to do just that. Remembering that our time is finite will give us the wisdom to make the most of this limited period. I felt this powerfully after the sudden death of my friend Bunty, to whom this book is dedicated.

Life has consequences. What we do matters. If you disagree, try playing with the opposite idea—that our life does not matter and what we do has no consequence. Which would you rather? Would you dare to make such a radical claim publicly at a funeral, or even privately, about your own life? In reality our day-to-day lives oscillate in a space between those two extremes. When we are confident and optimistic, how can life not hold great promise and opportunity? However, when disappointment or even disaster descends, how easily do we fall into despondency and despair.

Death is the great leveller. We try to ignore the reality of death. But if we can grasp its finality, we can find a way to accept with confidence a life moving towards this inevitable stage.

The Western-style secular view lacks any willingness to explore or accept the concept of anything more than this life. As Czeslaw Milosz described it, the true opium of the masses is not religion but the pervasive belief that this life is all there is.[170] We see that in books with titles such as *100 Things to Do before You Die*. The problem that belief creates is that there is only a finite amount of time within which we can experience all there is to experience. It creates, even at a subtle level, a sense of scarcity and fear that we are somehow missing out.

We live with deep longings and disappointments that this world can never seem to quite fulfil. These are the clues to the deep desires we have that can never seem to be satisfied. There are also profound implications for how we see what our life is about ultimately. Life offers more than what is going on around us. C. S. Lewis expands on this by affirming the Biblical claim that, as 'spiritual beings with a human existence', we have an eternal future ahead of us. Truly grasping that I am going to live forever puts into perspective that there are some things to which I need to pay relatively little attention and others requiring a great deal of attention. Take the example of an increasingly bad temper. If I live to the age of eighty, that bad temper may not be a particular problem. But if I am going to live for an infinite length of time, that bad temper will, over time, become a literal living hell for me. C. S. Lewis's far-reaching conclusion is:

> *Hell begins with a grumbling mood, always complaining, always blaming others, but you are still distinct from it. You may even criticise it in yourself and wish you could stop it. But there may come a day when you can no longer. Then there will be no you left to criticise the mood or to even enjoy it, but just the grumble itself going on and on forever like a machine. It is not a question of God 'sending us' to hell. In each of us there is something growing, which will* ***be*** *Hell unless it is nipped in the bud.*[171]

The choices that we make in this life, what we choose to focus on and allow to dominate our thinking, have profound implications for the person that we become. The sobering realisation is that those choices will continue to dominate us into eternity.

This is the importance of legacy. Our lives are headed in one direction or another. We have the great luxury of being able to change this direction in order to grow into all that God has for us.

The alternative, a terrifying one, is to grow increasingly towards self-centredness or allowing our ego to dominate. Which will it be?

I first picked up *A Resilient Life* by Gordon MacDonald when I turned forty. Even though that seems a very long time ago, I still remember the profound impact that the book had on me then and continues to have now. At the time, I was confronting midlife questions and self-doubt about what I had achieved or, perhaps more accurately, not achieved in my life. It seemed to me that so many others had achieved much more, progressed further along the road of their calling and developed more mastery of their destiny. This is a dangerous way to think; it had all the ingredients of a typical midlife crisis.

But midlife doesn't have to be a crisis. It can also be the chrysalis of something more wonderful and beautiful. Many of us are like those caterpillars longing to be butterflies. We sense that we are capable of so much more than what we see in front of us or have achieved so far. But as we become older, it's easy to deny those longings as the mere foolishness of youth. It is easy to tell ourselves that our best years are now behind us and that we ourselves are 'over the hill'.

What I found so refreshing in Gordon MacDonald's book was the powerful challenging of those assumptions. There is a beautifully simple analogy that drew me into the book. Imagine the marathon runner, Gordon MacDonald says. (In my case I do indeed have to imagine it as I have never run such a distance!) The race—all twenty-six miles and 365 yards (or 42.2 kilometres if you prefer) is long, gruelling and tough. In spite of all these hard conditions, the runner plans to pace themselves correctly in order to finish the race with a sprint. They do not just hobble across the finish line— they aim to end with a final flourish, a joyful celebratory crescendo for all they have come to do so far. The resilience of this final flourish is a fitting tribute to all that has happened up to that point.

MacDonald defined 'the way of resilience' as 'going through adversity, coming out stronger so they are now an inspiration to others, getting better as time goes by'.

For someone who is getting older, that is enormously attractive! Resilience matters increasingly because, as we have been exploring in this book:

- We are living longer than previous generations.
- Our lives are much faster and more unpredictable.
- At any time of the day, we are struggling with choices.
- We are bombarded by distractions.
- We lack supportive relationships, and those we do have tend to be functional rather than deep and abiding.

In that context Gordon MacDonald's imperatives are challenging:

- Move ahead no matter what has happened or is happening.
- Finish what we start.
- Persevere in adversity.
- Push ourself to our potential.
- Live life more as a marathon than as a sprint.

MacDonald says, '*It makes little difference how fast you can run the 100 metres when the race is 400 metres long. Life is not a sprint; it is a distance run, and it demands the kind of conditioning that enables people to go the distance*'.[172]

Of course, we can be called to leave the race at any point. None of us knows when that might be; on 17 March 2014, I was painfully reminded of that. But if we focus on what we have control over, we, too, need to pace ourselves for the long haul. Here was the clincher for me. The marathon runner aims to end the race with a sprint. After all those miles of running, she aims to have enough reserve so that she can end with a final burst of energy.

MacDonald reflects on how many of the characters that God used in the Old Testament tend to be either very young or very old. Of the men and women who are later on in life, there are people like Abraham or Moses in their sixties, seventies and eighties. This point has encouraged me for years and excites me about the future. We should be pacing our lives for the long haul such that our most fruitful and productive years can be our later years—in our own sixties, seventies and eighties!

For a world that celebrates youth and looks with nostalgia on the past, that is a powerfully subversive idea. When this idea is tied in with a favourite quote of mine, we have a powerful manifesto for the future: '*In Christ, our bad things can turn out for good, our good things can never be lost, and the best is yet to come!*'[173]

Rather than slowing down into retirement, we realise that our best years are rising up in front of us. In some mysterious and wonderful way, He is creating a tapestry for the future from the good, and from bad and even ugly in our life.

What can make this even more powerful is realising that leaving the world, which we all ultimately have to do, speaks to an understanding that covers the very end of time and the end of the world. Now, that really is an all-encompassing subject! It would be hard to describe anything broader than that!

What will happen at the end of time? How will the world end? How will our lives end? Where is history heading to? Is there any sense or coherence about the complex and challenging world in which we live? That question has been the subject of Hollywood movies and popular science fiction novels down the ages. Popular movies and novels have a great role to play as good fun and escapism, but aside from that we have to get on with the predictably mundane as life unfolds. Could there be another narrative? What does the world's bestselling and, arguably, least read and understood book say about the end of the world?

The Bible reveals that heaven and the new creation will be so much more than a simple idea characterised by sitting on a cloud, playing a harp, singing endlessly or even going on one long holiday! Heaven isn't even our final destination when we die! It is only, as it were, a transit lounge for the new creation. In fact, the Bible makes clear that we don't even ascend to heaven! The new creation is heaven, at the end of time, coming down to earth.

The God I Don't Understand by Chris Wright addresses this:

> *The new creation will start with the unimaginable reservoir of all that human civilisation has accomplished in the old creation—but purged, cleansed, disinfected, sanctified and blessed... Think of the prospect! All human language, literature, art, music, science, business, sport, technological achievement—actual and potential—all available to us. All of it with the poison of evil and sin sucked out of it forever. . . Whatever it may be like, we can rest assured that, for those who are in Christ, anything that has enriched and blessed us in this life will not be lost, but infinitely enhanced in the resurrection and anything that we have not been able to enjoy in this life (because of disability, disease or premature death—or simply through the natural limitations of time and space) will be amply restored or compensated for in resurrection life.*[174]

How, then should we live? '*We are to live as people who not only have a future, but know the future we have and go out and live in the light of that future, in preparation for it and characterised by its values*'.[175]

There is much more that we could explore together, but the purpose of this book is to encourage you to hunger and thirst for the path of wisdom. With such rich answers to these Four Vital Questions, what could our quest for wisdom look like?

REVIEW QUESTIONS TO CONSIDER

1. What kind of person do I want to be?
2. Where do I find a balance between the serious and fun moments in my life?
3. What kind of work would add meaning to my life?
4. What legacy do I want to leave behind?

9
YOUR WISDOM QUEST

We are caterpillars longing to become butterflies.

—Anonymous

When I studied medicine, I knew nothing about coaching. I had been trained to work with what has been called 'the medical model'. In many respects, it is very useful: disease and illness do need treating. However, it is not the only way to look at life and the significant problems and challenges that we face. There are also therapists, cousellors and coaches.

Comparing us, as human beings, to our relationship with a car is helpful. A therapist, like a doctor, seeks to fix what is broken. A counsellor will help you find out why it got broken in the first place. In contrast to these two, a coach will take your 'car' that is working reasonably well and help you work out where you want to go with it. Coaching is the means of determining direction and purpose in our life and then finding the motivation, energy and skills to pursue this direction so it becomes a reality.

Most people lack clarity about where they are in their lives, where they want to go, or what they want to become. Over the years, I have developed a coaching programme that I take my clients through. It's the means by which I help them to penetrate the complexity in their lives in order to find clarity in who they sense they are called to be and what they discern that they are called to do.

We look at ten main interrelated dimensions of life:

- Spiritual—your connection with God
- Intellectual—your engagement with significant ideas that matter to you
- Emotional—your psychological health
- Physical—the health of your body
- Marital—your relationship with your spouse or significant other
- Parental—your relationship with your children, nephews, nieces and godchildren
- Social—your network of friendships
- Vocational—your profession
- Avocational—your hobbies
- Financial—the health of your finances

It's common for many driven individuals to make goals and plans to cover only one area of life. Even if those goals are realised, it's easy to be left with regret or disappointment because one or more of the other dimensions has been neglected.

If there is no plan it is easy to either be driven to or drift towards a destination that we never intended. How much better to design our life with clear intentions and purpose! Of course, in reality the unexpected and unplanned can happen. As the World War Two leader and subsequent American President Dwight Eisenhower said, '. . . plans are useless, while planning is indispensable'.[176] It is the process of planning that takes our minds to another level and opens us up to options and possibilities we might not previously have thought possible. The plans we initially laid out may change dramatically as we progress, but in many ways that doesn't matter. An imperfect plan that is executed is far better than a perfect plan that is never attempted. An important principle is to hold on to our plans lightly, while keeping close to the One who knows the future and all things.

This becomes a dance with the unexpected and unpredictable, while moving forward with intention and purpose.

The tool that I use with my clients is the seven-step Dancing With Wisdom Coaching Programme ™ which I have developed. From what I have been saying so far, you may think that it is somewhat contradictory for me now to suggest a seven-stage process after criticising the modern tendency to seek simple steps as a solution to our significant challenges! To some extent you are right, and you have clearly followed my thinking. However, the purpose of a staged process is to enable those with whom I work to understand the components that are necessary for truly walking in wisdom. The principles behind the programme are timeless. The different components may look simple but will take a lifetime to master—like mastering all the ramifications of moves in a game of chess,

Here are the seven main stages. While they are written in a sequence, they're more of a recurring spiral than one step following after the one before.

> *The great secret about goals and vision is not the future they describe, but the change in the present they engender.*
>
> —David Allen[177]

Confidential Analysis—Let's Get Real!

Much of our life is spent in our heads . . . fears, worries, doubts, negative thinking. A rule of thumb estimate is that we have as many as 40,000 thoughts in a single day. What do we do with all those thoughts? How do we decide which to keep and which to discard? How do we handle the fears and insecurities? What do people think of me? Is this idea or plan crazy or worth pursuing?

I provide a safe space to explore the morass of ideas going through our heads that we might feel unsafe about expressing openly. Our sessions are non-judgmental and provide a space for brainstorming and exploration without any sense of having to be committed to a single course of action. It sounds so simple. But, it is difficult to find a place for exploring and developing those thoughts and ideas at the back of our minds, so that they rise to the surface to be truly fleshed out. One of my favourite questions during this time is what Dan Sullivan calls the R-Factor Question®. R stands for relationship and asks, 'If we were sitting here together three years from today, what would need to have happened in your personal and professional life for you to feel immensely pleased with your progress?'[178]

The power of this question lies in it being focussed not so far in the future that it's unreachable but also not close enough for there to be any assumption about doing more of the same thing.

I've found this question immensely helpful in understanding someone's true goals and ambitions. Some people can talk about their future in this way for literally hours. We focus, in particular, on the dangers that they want to avoid, the strengths that they are looking to maximise and the opportunities they want to capture.

Options Builder—Let's dream and raise the roof!

What I have experienced as the other person opens up to me is that there are a few deeply held desires and longings about what they want to do and where they want their lives to go. Often they have been too nervous or hesitant to share these deep thoughts with anyone else. It's a true privilege and honour to hear someone say, 'I've never discussed this with anyone, not even my spouse'.

Like nurturing a small seed embedded in the soil, we work together to nurture this tiny germ of an idea into growing and developing. It is inspiring to see enthusiasm, excitement and zest for life beginning to take hold.

Unique Game Plan—Let's discover!

Having spent time looking at various options, it becomes important to make a decision and commit to a course of action. Will that course of action necessarily lead to success? We don't know, but until we try we can never find out. That's why we are on a 'quest'. The process of finding out is as much about becoming the person we are called to be as it is about the fulfilling and satisfying work we are looking to put at the centre of our lives.

This is a journey of discovery. We do not know where we are going or how the journey will evolve, but it is still exciting and enormously meaningful.

Accountability Framework—Let's protect what we discover!

Any journey of self-discovery is going to involve failure and set back. The temptation to throw in the towel and give up may be very strong. How can we learn from failure, rather than allowing failure to bring discouragement and abandoning our dreams? In order to learn from our setbacks, we need to develop internally the thinking and externally the relationship structures that will pull us in the right direction rather than thwart and inhibit our progress.

Personalised Solution—Let's raise our game!

A favourite verse in my favourite book is: '*For we are God's workmanship created in Christ Jesus to do good works He has prepared in advance for us to do*' (Ephesians ch2 v10).

The word for workmanship in the original is the word *poema*, from which we derive our word poem. We are literally a work of art that God is sculpting and moulding to create something beautiful and lasting.

The journey to get there is not easy, but with patience and perseverance it is possible. This is the 'quest' that we talk about—a long search for something that is difficult to find, or an attempt to find something which is elusive. As we have pointed out, the person you become is at least as important as the goals you seek to accomplish. In working towards this personalised solution, we need to ensure that there is the correct balance between being and doing.

Resiliency Advantage—Let's stay strong!

Resilience is the ability to not only overcome adversity but also to confront and survive challenges in such a way that we become stronger and an inspiration to others. Frederick Nietzsche famously said, 'What does not kill me only seeks to make me stronger'.[179] With so many challenges from so many different directions, how can we develop systems and processes in our life which ensure that in spite of anything that happens we are able to keep putting our best foot forward?

Learning Expander—Let's keep growing!

All healthy organisms and organisations grow. The essence of life is to keep growing. We do not stop after climbing one mountain, but continually strive towards future goals. We were created to learn new things and grow. Most people pursue learning through popular media or the opinions of others. What is the quality of this approach?

Once we grasp that we are called to grow, an entire ocean of possibilities opens up before us! To capture these opportunties we need to learn how to clarify our thoughts so that we can process our feelings from the perspective of making better and wiser decisions. Coaching can assist in making this possible. Coaching works through equipping us to clarify our thoughts and process our feelings so we are in a stronger place where we can make better decisions.

However, as I have sought to explain throughout this book, wisdom is not only about finding ways to change our circumstances in order to get what we want. To develop wisdom, we also need to develop a hunger for growth, which is more important than simply changing something about our lives.

In *Where Your Treasure Is* Eugene Peterson expresses this as:

> *When we grow, in contrast to merely change, we venture into new territory and include more people in our lives—serve more and love more. Our culture is filled with change; it's poor in growth. New things, models, developments, opportunities are announced, breathlessly, every hour. But instead of becoming ingredients in a long and wise growth, they simply replace. The previous is discarded and the immediate stuck in—until, bored by the novelty, we run after the next fad. Men and women drawn always to the new never grow up. God's way is growth not change.*[180]

I hope that intrigues you enough to explore a free resource that I have for you at drsunil.com/workbook.

REVIEW QUESTIONS TO CONSIDER

1. What fears and insecurities would I like to ease?
2. What dreams am I trying to achieve?
3. What have I learned from previous setbacks?
4. How can I build my strengths to conquer any future challenges?

10

YOUR NEXT BEST STEP

Live Life in Crescendo! Your Most Important Work Is Always Ahead Of You.

—Personal Motto of Stephen R. Covey.
(*The 3rd Alternative: Solving Life's Most Difficult Problems*)

One of the challenges with writing a book on wisdom is that it feels as though it is never done! There's always much more to explore and think about. Where should a line be drawn saying, 'Enough is enough'? It is, also, easy to be overwhelmed and even feel intimidated by others who have developed this topic more eloquently or deeply. That's certainly been the case with this book.

At the beginning, we talked about discovering, desiring, developing and deepening in wisdom. That is the ongoing quest to which we have to keep on returning until the day when we finally meet our Creator. Wisdom is more than having the right technique for good choices and decisions. It is about having the character of mind and heart that enables us to make the right choices when there are no obvious answers. At the same time, we do this while walking life in partnership with the living God.

This is the God who makes Himself freely available to us because of Jesus Christ's commitment to us through the cross. The ability to walk this life comes through the power of the Holy Spirit.

This quest for wisdom becomes more than a mere walk. It is also a dance in which we come to know and understand God, as well as others and ourself, in a way that becomes broader, deeper and richer. Life is more exciting and fulfilling. With advancing age we replace the risk of drifting into a life which becomes less meaningful and more mediocre, with one based on looking forward and ahead with greater expectation and anticipation.

A great example of this is Charles Simeon.[181] In 1836, he retired after fifty-four years as a church minister at Holy Trinity Church in Cambridge, England. All accounts indicate that this godly man had lived a remarkable life of accomplishment, faithful service and fulfilment. He had achieved more than many church leaders of his time. Yet a friend discovered that this elderly man was still rising at four every morning to light his own fire, to spend time reading the Bible, praying in repentance and enjoying time with God. His friend, thinking that this was somewhat excessive, pleaded. 'Mr. Simeon, do you not think that, now that you are retired, you might take things more easily'? 'What?' replied the old churchman, 'Shall I not run with all my might now that the winning-post is in sight?'

Tim Keller reflected and interpreted this account of Charles Simeon for his own and our lives. Where he refers to spiritual disciplines, he could be referring to this quest for wisdom in our lives:

> *I am neither of advanced age nor a young man, but I know why Simeon could not imagine taking things "more easily." It was because the praising, the hoping, and the resting becomes better and better if you are willing to give it daily attention for years and years. The one hundredth time through the Psalms or the Proverbs will yield astonishingly sweet, comforting, and convicting insights, because*

> *the more you know the Bible as a whole the more sense do its particular parts make. And the more you know your own heart the more you know how to work on it, how to move past your discouragement, your peevishness, and your self-pity. But it takes years of relentless discipline. It is similar to how it takes years of practice to enjoy the power of playing the piano beautifully, but what we are talking about goes beyond even that in complexity and depth. When it comes to the spiritual disciplines, don't be a sprinter. Be a long-distance runner.*[182]

What an example of living life in crescendo! It is the recognition that our existence is finite and that through our faith we look to a greater and richer future in the life to come. This begins to assist us understand much of the incompleteness that we can feel. It is the realisation that no matter what we might achieve or do, there will always be a sense of incompleteness or of more that we could accomplish. How much more so is this the case in a world where we can always do something more, and our lists of what to do increase exponentially!

One person who struggled with this sense of incompleteness was the author J. R. R. Tolkien. He would go on to write one of the greatest fantasy novels of the twentieth century. During World War II he found himself contemplating death. It was far from clear whether he would live through such chaotic times or die without finishing his life's work. The thought of not knowing and the real possibility that he might never finish troubled him deeply. As a way of processing his fears, Tolkien found himself writing a short story about a man named Niggle.[183] The name Niggle is, in of itself, telling as it means '*to work . . . in a fiddling or ineffective way . . . to spend time unnecessarily on petty details*'.[184]

Niggle was an artist who was always getting distracted from his work. Being a good-natured person, he found neighbours and friends constantly asking favours of him that took away his time and attention. As the date came closer for his long journey (the metaphor Tolkien uses for death), Niggle worried he might never finish his greatest work, the painting of a tree. When the time for his departure arrived, Niggle took a last look at his painting to see that it was as he feared. He saw an unfinished work. All that his efforts had produced was a small leaf and a few relatively minor details. The rest of the painting that he had hoped to complete had never come to fruition. All of us can feel such regret; the unhappiness of leaving projects undone and fearing that we will never return to them. But Tolkien gives a poetic twist to his story. When Niggle completes his journey into the afterlife, he is taken aback by what he sees. Awaiting him, in all the glory that he had imagined in his mind, is the tree that he had never been able to finish! The work that was not completed in this life was finished in the next.

A common fear that many of us have to face is that of dying with important work still left undone and without a chance of expressing it to the world. Bunty's sudden death left me and many others with a great sense of incompleteness. Bunty was on the verge of doing something of real meaning and importance with his life. Whatever the reason may have been, that future was taken away. Such a sudden tragic loss always leaves a heavy sense of missed opportunity. But we have to accept and let go this sense of being unfinished. We have to come to terms with what will not be resolved, at least not in this life. That is what Niggle learned. In our life and quest for wisdom, there will be things we will not accomplish. But we can continue trying until we die, confident that in Christ the best is yet to come. The challenge for us is to do our work well, while not necessarily seeing the result.

I would like to close with this prayer from the American political commentator and theologian Reinhold Niebuhr. The first part of the prayer is very famous. I have seen it on walls in hospitals, clinics and waiting rooms all over the world:

> *God, give us grace to accept with serenity the things*
> *that cannot be changed,*

Courage to change the things which should be changed,
And the wisdom to distinguish the one from the other.[185]

However, for some reason the rest of the prayer is omitted. That is a huge disservice to us. It summarises much of what this quest for wisdom is about. The prayer continues:

Living one day at a time,
Enjoying one moment at a time
Accepting hardship as the pathway to peace
Taking, as Jesus did,
This sinful world as it is,
Not as I would have it,
Trusting that you will make all things right,
If I surrender to your will,
So that I may be reasonably happy in this life
And supremely happy with you forever in the next.[186]

The reminder to live one day at a time takes us back to this walk in wisdom, one step or day at a time. It is in the here and now, the sacrament of the present moment described as '*the sacred intoxication of existence*'.[187] It's a marvel and wonder that we are given yet another day to carry on! We accept that there are deeper truths and mysteries beyond our present awareness that can one day make sense of the hardships that we may well be experiencing in the present moment. As a result, rather than wishing we were somewhere else doing something different, we embrace this world with all its imperfection. We trust in surrender to our all-knowing God, realising He will eventually bring a deeper level of peace and joy into our lives. Beyond the present we look, with joyful anticipation, to the fulfilment and culmination of all things at the end of time.

Now that we have reached the end of this book, I want to thank you for joining me on this journey, or I should say 'quest'. We have defined a quest as a long search for something that's difficult to find or an attempt to achieve something that can only be done with difficulty. Through this book, I've taken you on my own personal quest to understand and grow in wisdom. I've attempted to show you areas in your own life where you, too, can find wisdom. While on the one hand it may be difficult, I trust that, on the other hand, this book will have made it a little easier or clearer for you.

You can obtain more resources from my blog at drsunil.com and iTunes at my podcast *Dancing With Wisdom (Making Sense of Life)'.*

As a reader of this book, I would like also to give you a gift to help you on your own quest for the best life that you are called to. Simply go to drsunil.com/workbook for more details.

How can we know that this book has served its purpose? If this book has made you hunger and thirst for wisdom and the God who exceeds our capacity to measure and control, while causing us to dance on the edge of mystery and glory, then I will have succeeded.

Welcome to this Dance with Wisdom!

'FINAL TRIBUTE'

This world is a great sculptor's workshop. We are the statues and there is a rumour going round the shop that some of us some day are going to come to life.

—C. S. Lewis

This book is dedicated to the memory of Abhishek Banerjee (Bunty), who I had the privilege of knowing for ten years and with whom I would have loved to have shared the lessons of this book. It seems fitting for me to end with something of the quest that our friendship took us on.

I first met Bunty in 2004 through our church at the time in Hounslow, West London. He had come from India to work at Metropolitan University on a master's degree in sports management.

Bunty was one of the fittest people I have ever known. He had amazing self-discipline for taking regular exercise, particularly weight training. He was meticulous with his routines and diet. He inspired me to take up a regular swimming routine and to make my physical health an important priority in my life.

Although knowing a lot of the Bible from childhood, it was on coming to England and meeting with other disciples of Christ that Bunty himself had a spiritual awakening. I had the privilege of baptising him in the summer of 2005. The Bible verse that God laid on my heart for him at the time—and that we discussed on a number of subsequent occasions—says, '*Have nothing to do with godless myths and old wives' tales; rather train yourself to be godly. For physical training is of some value, but godliness has value for all things, holding promise for both the present life and the life to come*' (The First Letter of Paul to Timothy ch 4 v7-8).

What were some of Bunty's qualities that I and so many others greatly appreciated?

1. His faithful friendship

Bunty enjoyed friends for friendship's sake. He had a wealthy abundance of close friends. In a world where so many see friendships as a means only to get a job done, Bunty was always willing to make himself available to talk and listen—no matter what the day or time. In the providence of God, I had gone to Delhi in what was to be the last week of his life. As was so typical of him, he'd go out of his way to pick me up from various addresses to take me to where I was staying in order that we could simply 'hang out' (as he liked to say) and chat. When I let him know about a relative's wedding in Mumbai later in the year that I was thinking about going to, he was keen that our two families drive over to Goa for a few days. Bunty understood that true success is related to friendships and community.

2. His sense of humour

Bunty had the uncommon skill of not taking himself too seriously. He took God seriously in his life but was able to easily find the funny side of the mundane or irritating. His one-liners and playful teasing of others brought so many of us joy and light relief. He was able to touch a heart skilfully before asking for a hand.

3. His generous spirit, servant heart and willingness to go the extra mile

Bunty gave a great deal of his time and effort for others. He had great talent, both musically and with technology. At the age of eighteen he went to St. Xavier's College in Mumbai. He would immerse himself for days at a time in organising the logistics for school performing arts productions. He loved the teamwork and camaraderie of working together behind the scenes toward a common goal. Bunty loved to see excellence in any activity and would always strive towards that goal.

At my home, I used to ask for his help regularly with challenges from my computer and electronic devices. I would find them enormously frustrating and draining. I recall Bunty regularly dealing with one of these technical challenges and when he saw that the computer was not doing what it was supposed to do, responding with 'That is really amazing! Wonderful!' His love of fixing things gave him enormous pleasure as a way to serve others.

Bunty was the first to help me grasp the potential in harnessing the power of technology. With the arrival of MP3 players and the iPod, he helped me to grasp the staggering potential and versatility of these new devices. I have on my iPod a folder that he made for me of his favourite worship songs. It is entitled simply *Bunty Album*. Two of those songs that I know he really loved are 'Who Am I?' and 'In Christ Alone'. I cannot hear those songs now without thinking of Bunty.

When I was with him in what was to be the last week of his life, I casually mentioned that my daughter Nisha was interested in photography. The next day, he spontaneously offered his SLR camera and equipment to Nisha, explaining that he no longer needed them. That was such a typical gesture, inspired by his generous nature.

4. His refusal to give in to negative circumstances

Bunty had an uncommon knack of looking to the positive and not giving in to destructive criticism or complaining. His manner of going out of his way to show appreciation to others was a real example to me. He instinctively understood the importance of the right attitude, no matter what the circumstances.

I know Bunty would be embarrassed by all that I'm writing about him here; he hated having attention drawn to him. But his caring nature and sensitivity were enormously enriching to so many of our lives.

I don't want to make out that Bunty was perfect—far from it. He knew that, as did his wife Jayshree, his friends and the rest of the family. Bunty and I spent many occasions discussing and praying about areas of his life where he was struggling. I was able to reciprocate his open honesty by sharing with him what I was finding difficult or challenging in my own life.

I know that Bunty's source of confidence and security was his personal relationship with Christ. It was where he placed his trust, and hope. All this rose above his own self-discipline. Huge as that was, he knew that it was not enough. Bunty knew that there is someone else who has lived the perfect life that we cannot live. He has gone to be with Him, Jesus.

Bunty still had much more to give this life. After his death Bunty's father shared with me how he appeared to be on the verge of major advancement and promotion in his career. As wonderful as that would have been, God had other ideas and we can only submit to His will.

Although he is no longer with us, I know that through his faith in Christ, he has gone to a much better place. He is content and at peace with God. It is we, his friends and family, who find it so hard.

Nevertheless, we do not grieve without hope. In Tolkien's *Lord of the Rings*, which Bunty enjoyed, Samwise Gamgee wakes up having been rescued from the fires of Mount Doom and sees Gandalf still alive. Samwise's words—because of Bunty's confidence in the resurrection—will become his as well. I know he would want us to experience this for ourselves. 'Gandalf, I thought you were dead. But then I thought I was dead. Is everything sad going to come untrue?'

Bunty knows that Jesus has made it possible for everything sad to become untrue. It is as though Bunty has gone to another room for which we, at the moment, do not have permission to enter. Bunty would want me to point you not to himself but to the resurrected Saviour, who has opened the door to eternal life and everlasting fulfilment.

He has got his unexpected promotion and is waiting for us there. We continue to miss him terribly but also know he is completely safe and secure. As someone who has had the privilege of knowing Bunty's heart, I'm sure he'd want you to know Christ's love, truth and grace in all its fullness, so that you, too, can know this ultimate security. Bunty understood how, as author Tim Keller expressed it, '*In Christ our bad things can turn out for good; our good things can never be lost and the best is yet to come*'.[188]

Bunty, I gave you a big hug to say goodbye that evening on Saturday, 15 March 2014. I look forward to getting another big hug when we meet again in eternity.

This is a book whose lessons I would have loved to have shared with you.

NOTES

BIBLICAL REFERENCES

I hope that *Dancing with Wisdom* will reach out to many who may not yet be familiar with the Bible. I have used a number of quotations, along with ones from other sources including authors such as C.S. Lewis and leading thinkers. I want the Biblical quotations to be as accessible as any from more contemporary sources that may be more familiar to those who are not acquainted with the Bible.

The detailed indication of the chapter and verse in the Bible is particular to religious texts, of most forms, and makes it easier for anyone studying them to find what they are looking for. I am aware, however, that to those who are not familiar with them, Biblical references can appear confusing, indeed daunting.

I have used a format which will, I hope, make it easier for you to follow up what I have included in *Dancing with Wisdom* by looking up the broader context in the Bible.

Let me explain with this reference: Proverbs ch 8 v10–11

'Proverbs' refers to the Book of Proverbs.

All books have a full title such as Book of Proverbs, Gospel of St Mark or First Letter of Paul to Timothy. They are also known by a shorter and more commonly used name, which for these books would be 'Proverbs', 'Mark' or 'Timothy'.

'ch' indicates the chapter. In this case Chapter 8

'v' shows the verse or verses, which are the shorter section of which the Chapter consists.

You can follow up on what I have written by looking for these Biblical extracts yourself. Google or any search engine will probably handle any version, but a frequently used format would show the reference above as: Proverbs. 8:10-11. 8 indicates the chapter; the numbers after the colon, 10-11, show the verses.

A helpful source is biblegateway.com.

SOURCE AND REFERENCES

I have used a number of quotes and sources to help you to understand about *Dancing with Wisdom*. Amongst many advantages is that this enables us all to benefit from the ability of others to encapsulate big ideas in short, memorable terms.

In the Notes and Bibliography at the end of the book, you will find more about the various sources I have used. I have tried to make the references and the Notes self-explanatory. However, I hope that you will be able to explore further, probably via the internet, both the people and the themes that we have been sharing in *Dancing with Wisdom*.

I want to make particular mention of three people whom I refer to regularly.

TIM KELLER

Tim Keller is an American pastor, theologian and prominent speaker. One of his themes is the importance of the spiritual health of urban populations. The church in New York which he grew to a weekly congregation of 5,000 is known for the unusually high participation of young professionals.

His talks and writing have been a major influence on both myself and those with whom I discuss the needs of our society. I had the honour of being his chauffeur when he visited London in 1999.

C. S. LEWIS

C. S. Lewis is well known as an English author, particularly of *The Chronicles of Narnia* and *The Screwtape Letters*. To date, the Narnia books have sold over 100 million copies and are a part of the canon of best-selling Christian books. He was, at different times, a member of the Oxford University Faculty of English—where he developed a strong friendship with J. R. R. Tolkien. He also held a chair of Medieval and Renaissance Literature at Cambridge University. He became a leading thinker on spiritual life and Christianity.

KING SOLOMON –'SOLOMON'

Solomon was a son of the most famous King of the Israelites, King David. He was also the last to rule over the United Kingdom of Israel, which fragmented after his death in 922 BC.

Solomon (970–931 BC) was the Biblical king most famous for his wisdom and perhaps best known for the Judgement of Solomon, which involved a dispute by two women over a child. He is credited with the Biblical books, Ecclesiastes, The Book of Proverbs and the Song of Solomon.

BIBLIOGRAPHY

1 David G. Blanchflower, "Is Happiness U-Shaped Everywhere? Age and Subjective Well-Being in 132 Countries," *NBER,* (January 10, 2020), Accessed April 23, 2020, https://www.nber.org/papers/w26641.

2 Thomas G. West and Plato, *Plato's Apology of Socrates: An Interpretation, with a New Translation*, 37e–38a, (Ithaca, N.Y.: Cornell University Press, 1979).

3 Theodore Roosevelt, *Theodore Roosevelt on Bravery: Lessons from the Most Courageous Leader of the Twentieth Century*, (New York: Skyhorse Publishing, 2015).

4 "What's Wrong with the World?" The Apostolate of Common Sense, The Society of Gilbert Keith Chesterton, April 29, 2012, https://www.chesterton.org/wrong-with-world/.

5 Friedrich Wilhelm Nietzsche, *Twilight of the Idols*, (Mineola, New York: Dover Publications, Inc., 2019).

6 Pierre Teilhard de Chardin, Julian Huxley, and Bernard Wall, *The Phenomenon of Man*, (New York: Harper & Brothers, Publishers, 1955).

7 C. S. Lewis (Clive Staples), *Mere Christianity*, (New York: Simon and Schuster, 1996).

8 Mary Oliver, "The Summer Day," *Poetry 180: A Poem a Day for American High Schools,* edited by Billy Collins, (Penguin Random House, 2001-2003).

9 Peter Walker, "Johnson Dodges LBC Radio Host's Questions about His Children," *The Guardian*, (November 29, 2019), https://www.theguardian.com/politics/2019/nov/29/boris-johnson-dodges-lbc-radio-hosts-questions-about-his-children.

10 Margaret Hartmann, "What Happened to the 20 Women Who Accused Trump of Sexual Misconduct?" *Intelligencer,* (February 26, 2019), https://nymag.com/intelligencer/2017/12/what-happened-to-trumps-16-sexual-misconduct-accusers.html.

11 "Projected Change in Global Population, 2015-2060," Pew Research Center's Religion & Public Life Project, (March 31, 2017), http://www.pewforum.org/2017/04/05/the-changing-global-religious-landscape/pf_17-04-05_projectionsupdate_changepopulation640px/.

12 ACL, "Interview with Dr. Ashley Null on Thomas Cranmer: Primary Author of the Book of Common Prayer," (Sydney, September 2001), http://acl.asn.au/old/null.html.

13 C. S. Lewis, *Surprised by Joy: The Shape of My Early Life,* (New York: Harcourt, Brace, Jovanovich, 1966).

14 Raphael Ben Levi, *Romance of the Hebrew Calendar*, quote attributed to Nahum 113 Month 1 Nisan/Aviv - first fruits - Yom Ha Bikkurim, (The Lockman Foundation, 1987).

15 William Shakespeare and Stephen Orgel, *Macbeth, Act 5, Scene 5,* (New York, New York: Penguin Books, 2016).

16 Lexico powered by Oxford "Carpe diem," Accessed on June 13, 2020.

17 C. S. Lewis, The Abolition of Man, or, Reflections on Education with Special Reference to the Teaching of English in the Upper Forms of Schools, (San Francisco: HarperOne, 2001).

18 Timothy Keller and Kathy Keller, God's Wisdom for Navigating Life: A Year of Daily Devotions in the Book of Proverbs, (New York, New York: Viking, 2017).

19 Oscar Wilde, Plays: Lady Windermere's Fan, (Harmondsworth: Penguin Books, 1974).

20 Timothy Keller, *Counterfeit Girls: The Empty Promises of Money, Sex, and Power, and the Only Hope That Matters*, (Penguin Books, Reprint Edition, October 4, 2011).

21 Cynthia Heimel, *If You Can't Live Without Me, Why Aren't You Dead Yet?* (New York: Grove Press, 2002).

22 Timothy Keller, *Counterfeit Girls: The Empty Promises of Money, Sex, and Power, and the Only Hope That Matters,* (Penguin Books, Reprint Edition, October 4, 2011).

23 Hannah Ritchie and Max Roser, "Urbanization," Our World in Data, June 13, 2018, https://ourworldindata.org/urbanization.

24 "Half the World Will Be Online in 2019," *The Economist*, https://www.economist.com/the-world-in/2018/12/31/half-the-world-will-be-online-in-2019.
25 Eric Teller in Thomas Friedman, *Thank You for Being Late: An Optimist's Guide to Thriving in the Age of Accelerations,* (Penguin, 2016).
26 Richard A. Swenson, *Margin: Restoring Emotional, Physical, Financial, and Time Reserves to Overloaded Lives,* (Colorado Springs: NavPress, 2014).
27 Adrian Paenza, "Exponential Growth: How Folding Paper Can Get You to the Moon," TED Talk, YouTube video, uploaded April 19, 2012. https://www.youtube.com/watch?v=AmFMJC45f1Q.
28 Ray Kurweil, "The Law of Accelerating Returns," Kurzweil Accelerating Intelligence, (March 7, 2001), https://www.kurzweilai.net/the-law-of-accelerating-returns.
29 Phil Akilade, "Digital is a Mindset," Issue #3, NKD Whistler, http://nkd.co.uk/wp-content/uploads/NKD_Digital-is-a-mindset_Whitepaper_web_v1.0.0.pdf.
30 WHO, "Depression," (January 30, 2020), https://www.who.int/news-room/fact-sheets/detail/depression.
31 "Ten Great Reasons to Give to Charity," *The Life You Can Save*, accessed March 15, 2019, https://www.thelifeyoucansave.org/learn-more/why-donate#collapseFAQs.
32 E91, "Thank God for the Complexities of Life," Blog, Accessed June 14, 2020, https://www.east91st.org/blog/thank-god-for-the-complexities-of-life/
33 Wikipedia, *The Free Encyclopedia*, "Uncertainty Principle," (Accessed June 6, 2020), https://en.wikipedia.org/wiki/Uncertainty_principle
34 Richard A. Swenson, *Margin: Restoring Emotional, Physical, Financial, and Time Reserves to Overloaded Live,* (Colorado Springs: NavPress, 2014).
35 Peter F.Drucker, *Classic Drucker: Essential Wisdom of Peter Drucker from the Pages of Harvard Business Review,* (Boston: Harvard Business Press, 2008).
36 Wikipedia, *The Free Encyclopedia*, "Facebook," (Accessed June 10, 2020), https://en.wikipedia.org/wiki/Facebook
37 Wikipedia, *The Free Encyclopedia*, "Kodak," (Accessed June 10, 2020), https://en.wikipedia.org/wiki/Kodak

38 Kenneth Negus, *Producing Pop: Culture and Conflict in the Popular Music Industry*, (London: E. Arnold, 1992): 21,

39 Roy B. Zuck, *The Speaker's Quote Book: Over 5,000 Illustrations and Quotations for all Occasions,* (Grand Rapids, MI: Kregel Academic & Professional, 2009).

40 Proceedings of the Third American Road Proceedings of the Third American Road Congress under the Auspices of American Highway Association and American Automobile Association, (Detroit, Michigan: September 29–October 4, 1913). Congress under the Auspices of American Highway Association and American Automobile Association, (Detroit, Michigan: September 29–October 4, 1913).

41 Lib Quotes, "According to the Oxford Dictionary of Humorous Quotations (Oxford University Press, 2013): 63, this quote is not verified and it has been stated by IBM to derive from a misunderstanding of an occasion, on 28 April 1953, when Thomas Watson Jnr. informed a meeting of IBM stockholders that 'we expected to get orders for five machines, we came home with orders for 18'." https://libquotes.com/thomas-j-watson.

42 Lib Quotes, "In a talk given to a 1977 World Future Society meeting in Boston. Olsen later explained that he was referring to smart homes rather than personal computers. Cited from 'Ken Olsen,'" Snopes, https://libquotes.com/search/?q=Ken+Olsen.

43 Steve Jobs and George W. Beahm, *I, Steve,* (Melbourne, Vic: Hardie Grant, 2011): 64.

44 Hunter Davies, *The Beatles: The Only Authorized Biography,* (London: Arrow Books, 1992).

45 Teri Pous, "Heart and Brain Surgery—Never Gonna Happen," *Time*, October 21, 2011, http://content.time.com/time/specials/packages/article/0,28804,2097462_2097456_2097329,00.html#:~:text=%22The%20abdomen%2C%20the%20chest%20and,to%20Queen%20Victoria%2C%20in%201873.

46 Edmond I. Eger, Lawrence J. Saidman, and Rod Westhorpe, The Wondrous Story of Anesthesia, (New York, NY: Springer, 2014).

47 Peter F. Drucker, *Innovation and Entrepreneurship: Practice and Principles*, (New York: Harper Business, 1985).

48 Kary Oberbrunner, *The Deeper Path: A Simple Method for Finding Clarity, Mastering Life, and Doing Your Purpose Every Day.* (Powell, Ohio: Author Academy Elite, 2008).

49 Stephen R. Covey, James C. Collins, and Sean Covey, *The 7 Habits of Highly Effective People: Powerful Lessons in Personal Change,* (New York : Simon & Schuster, 2020).

50 Richard A. Swenson, *Margin: Restoring Emotional, Physical, Financial, and Time Reserves to Overloaded Lives,* (Colorado Springs: NavPress, 2014).

51 Eric Schmidt, Center for Data Science College of Information and Computer Science, University of Massachusetts, (Accessed on June 27, 2020), http://ds.cs.umass.edu/eric-schmidt-google, as cited from "The Big Data Guru with Bernard Marr," www.smartdatacollective.com.

52 Peter F. Drucker, "Managing Knowledge Means Managing Oneself," in: *Leader to Leader,* 16, Spring 2000: 8–10.

53 Joel Hoomans, "35,000 Decisions: The Great Choices of Strategic Leaders," *Leading Edge Journal: Roberts Wesleyan College, Accessed June 11, 2020.*

54 Etymonline, "Decide," (Accessed 6-24-20), https://www.etymonline.com/search?q=decide.

55 Shai Danziger, Jonathan Levav, and Liora Avnaim-Pesso, "Extraneous Factors in Judicial Decisions," *Proceedings of the National Academy of Sciences* 108, no. 17 (2011): 6889-6892.

56 Ed Yong, "Justice is Served, But More So after Lunch: How Food-Breaks Sway the Decisions of Judges," *Discover Magazine* (2011).

57 John Hindley, *Dealing with Disappointment: How to Find Joy When Life Doesn't Feel Great,* (The Good Book Company, January 16, 2017).

58 Henry David Thoreau and Roderick MacIver, *Thoreau and the Art of Life: Reflections on Nature and the Mystery of Existence,* (Berkeley, Calif: North Atlantic Books, 2010).

59 Jonny Wilkinson and Steve Black, *Tackling Life: Striving for My Type of Perfection,* (London: Headline, 2009).

60 Mary Anne Layden, Ph.D., Center for Cognitive Therapy, Department of Psychiatry, University of Pennsylvania, (Testimony for U.S. Senate Committee on Commerce, Science and Transportation, November 18, 2004), as cited by Marripedia, "Effects of Pornography on Marriage," http://marripedia.org/effects_of_pornography_on_marriage#:~:text=The%20

estrangement%20between%20spouses%20wrought,a%20third%20lose%20their%20jobs.
61 Steven Stack, Ira Wasserman, and Roger Kern, "Adult Social Bonds and Use of Internet Pornography," *Social Science Quarterly* 85, no. 83, (2004): 75-88, as cited by Marripedia.org, http://marripedia.org/effects_of_pornography_on_marriage#:~:text=The%20estrangement%20between%20spouses%20wrought,a%20third%20lose%20their%20jobs.
62 Magdalena Mattebo, Tanja Tydén, Elisabet Häggström-Nordin, Kent W. Nilsson, and Margareta Larsson, "Pornography Consumption and Psychosomatic and Depressive Symptoms among Swedish Adolescents: A Longitudinal Study," *Upsala Journal of Medical Sciences* 123, no. 4 (2018): 237-246.
63 John Hindley, *Dealing with Disappointment: How to Find Joy When Life Doesn't Feel Great*, (The Good Book Company, January 16, 2017).
64 Henry David Thoreau, *Walden, or, Life in the Woods; and, On the Duty of Civil Disobedience*, (New York: Simon & Schuster Paperbacks, 2009).
65 Brené Brown, "Listening To Shame," TED Talk, YouTube, Uploaded March 16, 2012, https://www.youtube.com/watch?v=psN1DORYYV0.
66 Ronda Devereaux, *Understanding and Combating Fear, Choice Life Strategies*, January 17, 2013, http://choicelifestrategies.com/understanding-and-combating-shame/#:~:text=Think%20again%20%E2%80%93%20in%20her%20research,Trauma%2C%20Being%20Stereotyped%20or%20labeled.
67 Brené Brown, *Daring Greatly: How the Courage to Be Vulnerable Transforms the Way We Live, Love, Parent, and Lead,* (Penguin, January 17, 2013).
68 "Loneliness is a Serious Public Health Problem," CareMore Health, October 29, 2019, https://www.caremore.com/Media/News/2019/20191029-News-24FR.aspx.
69 "All the Lonely People: Loneliness Is a Serious Public-Health Problem," *The Economist, (September 1, 2018),* https://www.economist.com/international/2018/09/01/loneliness-is-a-serious-public-health-problem.
70 Julianne Holt-Lunstad, Timothy B. Smith, Mark Baker, Tyler Harris, and David Stephenson. "Loneliness and Social Isolation as

Risk Factors for Mortality: A Meta-Analytic Review." *Perspectives on Psychological Science* 10, no. 2 (2015): 227-237.

71 WebMD, "Stress Symptoms," Accessed June11, 2020, https://www.webmd.com/balance/stress-management/stress-symptoms-effects_of-stress-on-the-body#1.

72 Daniel R. Witte, D. E. Grobbee, Michiel L. Bots, and Arno W. Hoes, "A meta-analysis of excess cardiac mortality on Monday," *European Journal of Epidemiology* 20, no. 5 (2005): 401-406.

73 Etymonline, "Stress," (Accessed June 11, 2020), https://www.etymonline.com/word/stress.

74 Mark Jackson, Edmund Ramsden, and David Cantor, "Evaluating the role of Hans Selye in the modern history of stress," In *Stress, Shock, and Adaptation in the Twentieth Century*, University of Rochester Press, 2014.

75 Kelly McGonigal, "How to Make Stress Your Friend | Kelly McGonigal," TED, September 4, 2013, YouTube Video, 14:28, https://www.youtube.com/watch?v=RcGyVTAoXEU.

76 "National Press Club Seligman on positive psychology. A session at the National Press Club," *The General Psychologist* 34, no. 2, 1999, Summer): 37-45.

77 M. S. Reddy, "Depression: The Disorder and the Burden.' *Indian Journal of Psychological Medicine* 32, no. 1 (2010): 1.

78 Rudy V. Nydegger, *Understanding Therapy: How Different Approaches Solve Real-World Problems.* 2019, http://search.ebscohost.com/login.aspx?direct=true&scope=site&db=nlebk&db=nlabk&AN=2271460.

79 American Psychiatric Association, *Diagnostic and Statistical Manual of Mental Disorders: DSM-5.* (Arlington, VA: American Psychiatric Association, 2017).

80 *International Classification of Diseases 11th Revision,* World Health Organization, 2018, https://icd.who.int/en.

81 Christopher Dowrick and Allen Frances, "Medicalising Unhappiness: New Classification of Depression Risks More Patients Being Put on Drug Treatment from Which They Will Not Benefit." *Bmj* 347, (December 9, 2013), f:1740, doi:10.1136/bmj.f7140.

82 F. John Rey, "In Pursuit of Work and Life Balance," The Balance Careers, September 25, 2019, https://www.thebalancecareers.com/work-life-balance-and-juggling-glass-and-rubber-balls-

2275864https://www.thebalancecareers.com/work-life-balance-and-juggling-glass-and-rubber-balls-2275864.

83 Bronnie Ware, *Top Five Regrets of the Dying: A Life Transformed by the Dearly Departing*, (The. Carlsbad: Hay House Inc., 2019.)

84 Gordon MacDonald, *Ordering Your Private World*, (Nashville: W Publishing Group, 2017).

85 World Health Organization, "Suicide," September 2, 2019, https://www.who.int/news-room/fact-sheets/detail/suicide.

86 Scottye J Cash and Jeffrey A. Bridge, "Epidemiology of Youth Suicide and Suicidal Behavior," *Current Opinion in Pediatrics* 21, no. 5 (2009): 613.

87 Shaoni Bhattacharya, "Global Suicide Toll Exceeds War and Murder," *New Scientist,* (September 8, 2004), https://www.newscientist.com/article/dn6373-global-suicide-toll-exceeds-war-and-murder/.

88 Helen Schumacher, "Why More Men Than Women Die By Suicide," BBC Future: Psychology, https://www.bbc.com/future/article/20190313-why-more-men-kill-themselves-than-women.

89 "A National Investigation into Suicide by Children and Young People," University of Manchester: Manchester 1824, Accessed June 12, 2020, https://www.research.manchester.ac.uk/portal/en/projects/a-national-investigation-into-suicide-by-children-and-young-people(470da904-7d9e-46d7-903a-05e546404555).html.

90 Office for National Statistics, "Suicides in the UK: 2018 registrations," Accessed June 12, 2020, https://www.ons.gov.uk/peoplepopulationandcommunity/birthsdeathsandmarriages/deaths/bulletins/suicidesintheunitedkingdom/2018registrations.

91 Sinek, Simon, *Start with Why: How Great Leaders Inspire Everyone to Take Action*, (Portfolio; Reprint edition, December 27, 2011).

92 Czeslaw Milosz, "Discreet Charm of Nihilism," *New York Review of Books* 45, no. 18 (1998): 17.

93 Os Guinness, *Long Journey Home: A Guide to Your Search for the Meaning of Life*, (Colorado Springs: WaterBrook Press, 2001).

94 W. H. Auden and Edward Mendelson, *The Complete Works of W. H. Auden,* (Princeton, NJ: Princeton University Press, 1988.)

95 Gordon MacDonald, *A Resilient Life: You Can Move Ahead No Matter What,* (Nashville, Tennessee: Thomas Nelson, 2009), https://www.overdrive.com/search?q=43309761-833E-493D-921A-B086F661EA92.

96 "The Elder's Spiritual Life an Elder's Personal Life and Growth (3)," Bible Leadership, Accessed June 12, 2020, https://www.biblicaleldership.com/files/curriculum/personal_life_3_doutline.pdf.

97 Dorothy L. Sayers, "The Other Six Deadly Sins," Excerpt: Sloth, Lectionary Central, October 23, 1941, http://www.lectionarycentral.com/trinity07/Sayers.html.

98 Chris Laker, '"God Must Have a Very High Opinion of Me' - 51 of the Most Memorable Jose Mourinho Quotes," *Evening Standard*, January 25, 2014, https://www.standard.co.uk/sport/football/god-must-have-a-very-high-opinion-of-me-51-of-the-most-memorable-jose-mourinho-quotes-9075258.html.

99 John Newton and Josiah Bull, *Letters by the Rev. John Newton: of Olney and St. Mary Woolnoth, Including Several Never Before Published, with Biographical Sketches and Illustrative Notes,* (London: Religious Tract Society, 1869).

100 Attributed to William Law, as cited by David Marcum and Steven B. Smith, *Egonomics: What Makes Ego Our Greatest Asset (or Most Expensive Liability),* (Touchstone; Reprint edition, September 9, 2008).

101 Etymonline, "Ego," (Accessed June 12, 2020), https://www.etymonline.com/search?q=ego.

102 Jim Collins, *Good to Great,* (HarperCollins, 2011), http://api.overdrive.com/v1/collections/v1L2BaQAAAJcBAAA1M/products/acb8ff95-ca18-47d0-b0ed-cb3445a0ff22.

103 Bing Translator Powered by Oxford Dictionaries, "Ego," (Accessed June 12, 2020), https://www.bing.com/search?q=definition+of++ego&src=IE-SearchBox&FORM=IESR3A.

104 Bing Translator, Powered by Oxford Dictionaries, "Pride," (Accessed June 12, 20200, https://www.bing.com/search?q=definition+of++pride&qs=n&form=QBRE&sp=-1&pq=definition+of+pride&sc=6-19&sk=&cvid=D79EB79F599E4E0285B87AD914FA53E3.

105 C. S. Lewis (Clive Staples), *Mere Christianity,* (New York: Simon and Schuster, 1996).

106 Isak Dinesen, *Out of Africa,* (New York: Random House, 1938): 161.

107 Isak Dinesen, *Out of Africa,* (New York: Random House, 1938): 271.

108 Timothy Keller and Grover Gardner, *The Freedom of Self-Forgetfulness: The Path To True Christian Joy,* (Christian Audio, 2013).
109 Theodore Roosevelt, *Theodore Roosevelt on Bravery: Lessons from the Most Courageous Leader of the Twentieth Century,* (New York: Skyhorse Publishing, 2015).
110 Marshall Goldsmith, *Overcoming Ego*, YouTube, Uploaded August 16, 2016, also presented at https://www.drsunil.com/thinking/overcoming-ego/
111 Timothy Keller, *The Man the King Delights to Honor – Timothy Keller* [Sermon], YouTube, Uploaded by Gospel of Life on August 10, 2015, https://www.youtube.com/watch?v=oNBJqCFiDxw.
112 Albert Einstein, *The Einstein Reader,* (United Kingdom: Citadel, 2006).
113 C. S. Lewis (Clive Staples), *Mere Christianity*, (New York: Simon and Schuster, 1996).
114 Susanna Annesley Wesley, *Susanna Wesley: The Complete Writings*, (New York: Oxford University Press, 1997).
115 Etymoline, "Humility," (Accessed June 12, 2020), https://www.etymonline.com/search?q=humility.
116 Ralph W. Sockman, *Arkansas Methodist*, as cited by Editor Larry Chang, *Wisdom for the Soul: Five Millennia of Prescriptions for Spiritual Healing,* (United States: Gnosophia Publishers, 2006).
117 C. S. Lewis, The Screwtape Letters, (Las Vegas, Nevada: FAB, 2016), as quoted by Timothy Keller, *The Man the King Delights to Honor – Timothy Keller* [Sermon], YouTube, Uploaded by Gospel of Life on August 10, 2015, *https://www.youtube.com/watch?v=oNBJqCFiDxw.*
118 David Marcum and Steven B. Smith. *Egonomics: What Makes Ego Our Greatest Asset (or Most Expensive Liability),* (New York, NY: Touchstone, 2018).
119 C. S. Lewis (Clive Staples), *Mere Christianity*, (New York: Simon and Schuster, 1996).
120 "Why Is the Owl Considered a Wise Bird in the West and a Symbol of Foolishness in India?" *Times of India*, October 3, 2004, https://timesofindia.indiatimes.com/Why-is-the-owl-considered-a-wise-bird-in-the-West-and-a-symbol-of-foolishness-in-India/articleshow/871894.cms#:~:text=In%20India%2C%20the%20owl%20is,is%20attained%20by%20foul%20means.&text=

When%20shown%20travelling%20on%20an,symbol%20of%20corruption%20of%20wealth.
121 Wikipedia, *The Free Encyclopedia*, "Wesley Covenant Service," (Accessed June 13, 2020), https://en.wikipedia.org/wiki/Wesley_Covenant_Service.
122 Isak Dinesen, *Out of Africa*, (New York: Time Incorporated, 1963).
123 Martin Luther, *The Table Talk of Martin Luther*, (H. G. Bohn, 1857).
124 "Wikitionary, "ἐπιθυμία, (Accessed June 13, 2020), https://en.wiktionary.org/wiki/%E1%BC%90%CF%80%CE%B9%CE%B8%CF%85%CE%BC%CE%AF%CE%B1#:~:text=yearning%2C%20longing%2C%20desire%2C%20craving,with%20a%20negative%20connotation%3A%20lust
125 David Foster Wallace, "This Is Water," *Alumni Bulletin*, Kenyon College, Accessed May 14, 2020, http://bulletin-archive.kenyon.edu/x4280.html.
126 David Foster Wallace, "This Is Water," *Alumni Bulletin,* Kenyon College, Accessed May 14, 2020, http://bulletin-archive.kenyon.edu/x4280.html.
127 C. S. Lewis (Clive Staples), *Mere Christianity,* (New York: Simon and Schuster, 1996).
128 C. S. Lewis (Clive Staples), *Mere Christianity,* (New York: Simon and Schuster, 1996).
129 C. S. Lewis and Julian Rhind-Tutt, *The Weight of Glory*. ([United States]: Harper Collins Publishers, 2014), https://www.hoopladigital.com/title/11589113.
130 Thomas Chalmers, "The Expulsive Power of a New Affection," https://www.monergism.com/thethreshold/sdg/Chalmers,%20Thomas%20-%20The%20Exlpulsive%20Power%20of%20a%20New%20Af.pdf.
131 Mark Twain, "Never Let Schooling Interfere with Your Education," Quote Investigator, Accessed June 13, 2020, https://quoteinvestigator.com/2010/09/25/schooling-vs-education/.
132 Francis Chan, *Crazy Love: Overwhelmed by a Relentless God,* (Colorado Springs, CO: David C. Cook, 2013).
133 ACL, "Interview with Dr. Ashley Null on Thomas Cranmer: Primary Author of the Book of Common Prayer," (Sydney, September 2001), http://acl.asn.au/old/null.html.

134 Eugene H. Peterson, *God's Message for Each Day: Wisdom from the Word of Go,* (Nashville, TN: Thomas Nelson, 2006).
135 C. S. Lewis, *Christian Reflections,* (Grand Rapids, MI: W. B. Eerdmans, 2014).
136 Eugene H. Peterson, *Where Your Treasure Is: Psalms that Summon You from Self to Community*, (Grand Rapids, MI: W. B. Eerdmans, 1993).
137 C. S. Lewis, *A Year with C. S. Lewis: 365 Daily Readings from His Classical Works*, (New York, NY: William Collins, 2013).
138 Richard Dawkins, *The God Delusion*, (Boston, MA: Mariner Books, 2008).
139 Blaise Pascal, *Thoughts*, Editor Charles W. Eliot, LL D, Translated by W. F. Trotter, M. L. Booth, and O.W. Wight, Harvard Classics, (New York: F. F. Collier and Son, 1917).
140 Timothy-Dudley Smith, "As Water to the Thirsty," Hymnary, Accessed June 13, 2020.
141 Brad Price, *Romans Bible Commentary - Living By Faith,* (Publisher: www.abiblecommentary.com, December 2005).
142 Daniel Goleman, *Emotional Intelligence: Why It Can Matter More Than IQ,* (New York City, NY: Bantam, 2005).
143 D. M. Welton, "The Old Testament Wisdom (Chokma)," *The Biblical World* 10, no.3 (University of Chicago Press, September 1897): 183-189
144 Timothy Keller, *The Way of Wisdom: A Year of Daily Devotions in the Book of Proverbs*, (London: Hodder & Stoughton Ltd, 2019).
145 BibleHub, "Hebel," found in Strong's Concordance, (Accessed June 14, 2020), https://biblehub.com/hebrew/1892.htm.
146 Etymonline, "Satan," Accessed June 14, 2020, https://www.etymonline.com/search?q=Satan.
147 Randy Alcorn, *The Treasure Principle: Unlocking the Secret of Joyful Giving*, (Portland, OR: Multnomah Books, 2005).
148 Henry Cloud and John Sims Townsend, *Safe People: How To Find Relationships That Are Good for You and Avoid Those That Aren't,* (Grand Rapids, Michigan: Zondervan, 2016).
149 Timothy Keller, *God's Wisdom for Navigating Life*, (Viking, 2017).
150 Bruce K. Waltke, *The Book of Proverbs, Chapters 1–15,* (Grand Rapids, MI: W. B. Eerdmans, 2004).
151 Aleksandr Solženicyn and H. T. Willetts, *The Gulag Archipelago 3, no.3,* (New York: Harper & Row, 1978).

152 John C. Maxwell, *The 21 Irrefutable Laws of Leadership,* (Nashville, Tenn: Thomas Nelson, 2008).
153 John Maxwell, *The Law of the Inner Circle: Lesson 11 from the 21 Irrefutable Laws of Leadership,* (Nashville, TN: HarperCollins Leadership, 2012).
154 Henry Cloud and John Sims Townsend, *Safe People: How to Find Relationships That are Good for You and Avoid Those That Aren't,* (Grand Rapids, Michigan, Zondervan, 2013), http://www.OneClickDigital.com.
155 Henry Cloud, *Necessary Endings: The Employees, Businesses, and Relationships That All of Us Have to Give Up in Order to Move Forward,* (HarperCollins e-books, January 18, 2011).
156 Rebecca Manley Pippert, *Hope Has Its Reasons,* (Marshall Pickering, 1990).
157 Timothy Keller, *The Reason for God: Belief in an Age of Skepticism,* (New York, NY: Penguin Books, 2008).
158 Miroslav Volf, *Exclusion and Embrace: a Theological Exploration of Identity, Otherness, and Reconciliation* (Nashville: Abingdon Press, 2019), *https://public.ebookcentral.proquest.com/choice/publicfullrecord.aspx?p=5844697.*
159 Timothy Keller, *The Reason for God: Belief in an Age of Skepticism,* (New York, NY: Penguin Books, 2008).
160 Czeslaw Milosz, "Discreet Charm of Nihilism," *The New York Review of Books* 45 no. 18, (1998.): 17.
161 Dawson Trotman, *Personal Journal,* (Special Collections, The Navigators International Headquarters Archives, Colorado Springs, February 14, 1933), as cited by Jeffrey Paul Reynolds, Dawson Trotman's Personal Spiritual Disciplines As The Foundation For His Great Commission Ministry, The Southern Baptist Theological Seminary, https://repository.sbts.edu/bitstream/handle/10392/4859/Reynolds_sbts_0207D_10223.pdf?sequence=1&isAllowed=y.
162 Parker J. Palmer, *Let Your Life Speak: Listening for the Voice of V*ocation, (Jossey-Bass; 1 edition, May 18, 2009).
163 Martin Luther King and Coretta Scott King, *Strength to Love: Sermons from Strength to Love and Other Preachings,* (Boston, Mass: Beacon Press, 2019).
164 Lawrence Pearsall Jacks, *Education through Recreation,* (Washington: McGrath Pub. Co., 1972).

165 Timothy Keller and Katherine Leary Alsdorf, *Every Good Endeavour: Connecting Your Work to God's Plan for the World,* (London: Hodder & Stoughton 2014).
166 Timothy Keller and Katherine Leary Alsdorf, *Every Good Endeavour: Connecting Your Work to God's Plan for the World,* (London: Hodder & Stoughton 2014).
167 C. S. Lewis, *The Complete C. S. Lewis,* Signature Classics, (New York, NY: HarperCollins, 2007).
168 Keith and Kristyn Getty, Jeff Taylor, and Stuart Townend, "Before You I Kneel, (A Worker's Prayer)," from *Hymns for the Christian Life,* GettyMusic and Seek 1st Publishing (Adm. By Musicservices. Org) and Townend Music (Adm. UK & Europe By Thankyou Music, 2012).
169 Teresa, and Brian Kolodiejchuk. *Mother Teresa: Come Be My Light: The Private Writings of the 'Saint Of Calcutta,'* (Bangalore, India: Asian Trading Corporation, 2014. ©2007).
170 Wikipedia, "Opium of the People," (Accessed June 24, 2020), https://en.wikipedia.org/wiki/Opium_of_the_people#:~:text=ist%20das%20Opium%20des%20Volkes,the%20opiate%20of%20the%20masses.%22&text=The%20full%20quote%20from%20Karl,the%20soul%20of%20soulless%20conditions.
171 C. S. Lewis, *Mere Christianity,* (San Francisco, CA: HarperOne, 2015).
172 Gordon MacDonald, *A Resilient Life: You Can Move Ahead No Matter What,* (Nashville, Tennessee: Thomas Nelson, 2009), https://www.overdrive.com/search?q=43309761-833E-493D-921A-B086F661EA92.
173 Jonathon Edwards, "Because of Jesus, All Our Bad Things Turn Out for Good, All Our Good Things Can Never Be Lost and The Best Is Yet to Come," https://www.bible.com/events/2613585.
174 Christopher J. H. Wright and John R. W. Stott, *The God I Don't Understand: Reflections on Tough Questions of Faith,* (Zondervan, February 9, 2016).
175 Sunil Raheja, "The Literal End of the World?" Podcast 29, March 03, 2017, https://www.drsunil.com/spirituality/podcast-029-the-literal-end-of-the-world/
176 John Bartlett, Robert Andrews, Mary Biggs, and Michael Seidel, *Columbia World of Quotations,* (New York: Bartleby.com, 2001).

177 David Allen, *Making It All Work Winning at the Game of Work and the Business of Life* (East Rutherford: Penguin Publishing Group 2008), http://public.eblib.com/choice/PublicFullRecord.aspx?p=6080422.

178 Dan Sullivan, *The Dan Sullivan Question,* (The Strategic Coach, Inc., June 1, 2009).

179 Friedrich Wilhelm Nietzsche, *Twilight of the Idols*, (Lexington, KY: publisher not identified], 2014).

180 Eugene H. Peterson, *Where Your Treasure Is: Psalms that Summon You from Self to Community,* (Eerdmans; Reprint edition, November 3, 1993).

181 Timothy Keller, *My Rock; My Refuge: A Year of Daily Devotions in the Psalms*, (London: Hodder & Stoughton, 2017).

182 Timothy Keller, "Long Distance Spirituality," Blog, May 27, 2010, https://timothykeller.com/blog/2010/5/27/long-distance-spirituality

183 J. R. Tolkien, *Leaf By Niggle*, (Harper Collins, 2001).

184 Etymonline, "Niggle," Accessed June 14, 2020, https://www.etymonline.com/search?q=niggle

185 Fred R. Shapiro, "Who Wrote the Serenity Prayer?" *The Chronicle of Higher Education.* (April 28, 2014).

186 Wikipedia, The Free Encyclopedia "Serenity Prayer," (Accessed June 13, 2020), https://en.wikipedia.org/wiki/Serenity_Prayer

187 Ian Ker, G. *K. Chesterton: A Biography*, (Oxford: Oxford University Press, 2012), https://doi.org/10.1093/acprof:osobl/9780199601288.001.0001.

188 Timothy Keller, *Walking with God through Pain and Suffering*, (Riverside Books, 2013).

ACKNOWLEDGEMENTS

In the process of getting to publication, my friend Roger Randall shared a quote with me that "Writing a book is no more difficult than giving birth to barbed wire." I can entirely see how this can be the case, but the following people have ensured that the journey has also been punctuated with periods of joy, fun and even delight.

My dear wife Sally and our precious children Sonia, Nisha, Priya and Rohan for your patience and forbearance with me on this project that has taken way longer than I ever anticipated.

Mum and Dad for your practical support and encouragement over the years in far too many ways to count. Your consistent demonstration of unconditional love and forgiveness has meant so much to me.

To Bunty's wife, Jayshree, and his parents Rita and Nirmal for your friendship and love. We look forward to meeting Bunty again in eternity.

Andrew Horton for all your support and encouragement with the podcasts and blogs. Your behind the scenes technical expertise has been invaluable. Our podcast conversations and your penetrating questions have made podcasting so much fun and laid much of the foundation for this book.

Kary Oberbrunner and the Igniting Souls Tribe for helping make me believe I could write a book and cheering me on the way.

My amazing editors Tina Morlock, Diane Walters and John Clarke. Tina, your gentle encouragement and incisive questions helped me to keep on track and not lose direction. When I found myself drowning in way too many quotes, you helped me distil them down to what was most relevant. Diane, your attention to detail and ability to research references amazed me. You extended yourself beyond the call of duty and for that I am very grateful. John, our numerous conversations and forensic analysis of the text ensured that I could communicate what I wanted to say with so much greater clarity and precision. Thank you for your patience and perseverance with me.

Donna Cowan, your practical expertise on all things to do with publishing was such a life-line to me. Your positive can-do attitude and hearty affirming laughs on our Zoom calls made such a difference. When I felt myself getting overwhelmed, our calls were a breath of fresh air and huge encouragement.

Pete and Pat Gano for being willing for me to share early drafts and ideas when it was so unclear as to what I was saying and where I was going.

Rahil Patel for your willingness to keep pushing and prompting me to persevere during the early stages when I kept going round in circles was a vital part of the journey.

Emily Taylor your prayers and encouragement to keep pressing on made a real difference to my confidence that this project could actually get done. Knowing you were praying for me was a huge source of strength to me.

Dominic Hughes for being willing to read early drafts of the manuscript. Your enthusiastic recommendations to others inspired me to keep persevering.

Simon Lees for believing in the importance of the content and continual encouragement to make the writing clearer. You challenged me to better communicate the ideas and concepts so as to help as many people as possible. Thank you also for introducing me to John Clarke.

Paul Hawkins for your thoughtful reflections and feedback on earlier versions of the manuscript.

Steven Ho for our many conversations and your hunger to explore more of the ideas, inspiring me to keep going to help others.

Yvonne and Robert Done for all our many conversations and your willingness to think through how different parts of the material could be relevant to your own specific life circumstances. Your willingness to apply parts of the material in your own lives and seeing your personal transformation continues to be a wonderful privilege for me.

Bjorn and Joelle Lennard, your hunger to grow and develop along with applying the material in your own lives was a delight to witness.

Rico Tice, thank you for encouraging me to persevere and helping me to see how this message needs to be heard. Your giftedness in communicating truth in both a winsome and candid way continues to inspire me.

Kathleen Thompson for your encouragement to keep persevering on and helpful comments on an earlier draft.

Isaac and Gloria Shaw and the team at Delhi Bible Institute for all your support over the years and being so willing and appreciative in allowing me to test out my ideas in such a consistent way through conferences and workshops.

Karl Stott for your challenging and insightful questions on the blog over the years have sharpened my thinking and helped me think through many of the challenges of faith.

Julia Haviland who, from my appraisal, gave me permission to make this book a meaningful objective as well as believing in me and that I could actually complete it.

My Facebook support group and your willingness to play with the ideas and concepts.

David Jackman for being one of the first people to show me how it is possible to communicate truth in a loving manner.

Tim Keller whose talks, books and wisdom over the years have profoundly influenced my thinking.

Finally, if you do not see your name here, please forgive any oversight on my part.

ABOUT THE AUTHOR

Sunil is an author, blogger, podcaster and coach. It is his privilege to work with senior leaders who feel stuck—empowering them to re-engage with deeper purpose and live life in crescendo, so their best days are still to come.

Sunil has worked as a psychiatrist for over 25 years. He lives in London, England with his wife, Sally. They have four grown children.

Get your complimentary workbook that goes with this book at drsunil.com/workbook

THE DANCING WITH WISDOM COACHING PROGRAMME™

Define your unique path to meaning, purpose and fun!

You've read the book. Now where do you go from here?

Where do you sense your life is heading? Is that a direction you truly want to go?

Is the life you are living the same as the life that wants to live in you?

This book has been the first step in your quest. What about the rest of your journey?

If you are interested in continuing this quest for wisdom and building a meaningful legacy together with me, please visit drsunil.com/workbook for more in-depth training and resources to help you on your journey.

Let us together learn to live life in crescendo with our best years in front of us!

I am excited to see where this journey will take you!

Lightning Source UK Ltd.
Milton Keynes UK
UKHW021111100521
383424UK00004B/78